I just finished reading *7 Roadl* [...] terrific follow up to *7 Simple S*[...] book in the Hearing God's V[...]  communication with God. In this second book, she encourages and assists us in looking deeper within ourselves to see what may be limiting that communication. By sharing her personal struggles, she inspires us to continue the journey and not give up!—***Sandy S.***

Sindy Nagel speaks the language of a learner. From her heart, to the printed page, she has provided a path for you to walk deeper in your knowing of Jesus. May you discover yourself in these pages and find how dearly loved you are by Him.—***Pastor Bill Frisbie, Northwest Gathering Center, Coeur d'Alene, Idaho.***

7 Roadblocks to Hearing God Speak delivers an honest look at barriers that can exist and prevent us from hearing God. The author does a wonderful job in identifying these barriers and how we can avoid them. With this knowledge, the reader finds encouragement and hope, knowing that God does speak to us and is always with us.—***Julie L.***

Once again, Sindy Nagel provides a clear and straightforward path to a deeper and more satisfying prayer life. Her books are essential to all prayer warriors!—***Craig Witcher, Founder, Manna Ministries Worldwide and Manna Café.***

Sindy captures your interest and attention right away. Her insight leads you to examine your thoughts and actions to enable you to hear God speaking to you.—***Sandra V.***

Sindy did it again! She proved that she "can do all things through Christ Who gives her strength." Through her humility, she heard God's voice and shared that gift with her readers. I just know this book will reach people who are struggling to hear God's voice and help them bust through the roadblocks with amazing speed (results)! May the Lord bless all those who believe the truths and apply the principles offered in this book.—***Sally W.***

What wonderful, Biblical truths come from *7 Roadblocks to Hearing God Speak*. Sindy has again listened to the Lord speak to her and given those inspired words to each one of us. Read on and learn how you, too, can hear God speak!—***Shelly B.***

Hearing God's Voice Series

(Book 2)

7 ROADBLOCKS TO

Hearing God Speak

REMOVING THE BARRIERS BETWEEN YOU AND GOD

SINDY NAGEL

Copyright © 2016 Sindy Nagel

All Rights Reserved

Copyright © 2016 Sindy Nagel. All rights reserved. No part of this book may be used or reproduced by any means, graphic, electronic, or mechanical, including photocopying, recording, taping, or by any information storage-retrieval system, without the written permission of the author, Sindy Nagel, except in the brief quotations embodied in critical articles and reviews. Do not sell this book in any form for personal gain.

Scriptures taken from the Holy Bible, New International Version®, NIV®. Copyright © 1973, 1978, 1984, 2011 by Biblica, Inc.™ Used by permission of Zondervan. All rights reserved worldwide. www.zondervan.com. The "NIV" and "New International Version" are trademarks registered in the United States Patent and Trademark Office by Biblica, Inc.™

The NIV Bible does not capitalize the God pronouns. However, the author capitalized all God pronouns (i.e. He, His, Him, Himself, etc.) in all Bible verses and quotes listed in this book in order to give our awesome God the honor and glory He deserves.

ISBN: 978-0-9969934-6-3 (Paperback)
ISBN: 978-0-9969934-9-4 (Kindle)
ISBN: 978-0-9969934-2-5 (Audio Book)

Edited by Monique Bos

Cover design by Angela Ayala from www.fiverr.com.

Author photo on back cover by Wendy Swenson Photography.

Photos for cover design purchased from www.depositphotos.com: 1) Asphalt road in green fields under beautiful sky ©Timmary, 2) Barricade and warning light closeup © flashon.

Photos for interior purchased from www.depositphotos.com: 1) LIE red rubber stamp vector over a white background © gorkemdemir, 2) TRUTH © chrisdorney, 3) BIBLE Holy bible book with cross isolated on white © Alexmit.

Printed in the United States of America.

Dedicated to

My Immanuel

Who calms my fears, saying,

"I will never leave you or forsake you…
Be strong and very courageous…
Have I not commanded you? Be strong and courageous.
Do not be terrified; do not be discouraged,
for the LORD your God will be with you
wherever you go." (Joshua 1:5, 7, 9)

Contents

Good News ix
Preface xv

Introduction 1
Chapter 1 – DOUBT, The Enemy of Belief 5
Chapter 2 – FEAR, The Enemy of Confidence 44
Chapter 3 – PRIDE, The Enemy of Humility 82
Chapter 4 – WORRY, The Enemy of Trust 108
Chapter 5 – BUSYNESS, The Enemy of Freedom 134
Chapter 6 – DISOBEDIENCE, The Enemy of Righteousness 159
Chapter 7 – UNWILLINGNESS TO FORGIVE, The Enemy of Mercy 199
Conclusion 224
Thank You! 226

Good News

When you seek God with all your heart, you will find Him! To hear God's voice regularly, you need to be in a close relationship with Him. The journey to greater intimacy with Jesus begins with acknowledging your sin. The God of all creation is righteous and holy. He doesn't want to be near immorality. So our disobedience, rebellion, and sin separate us from Him. Sin is anything that doesn't please God. It's not just committing one of the big ten, like: murder, adultery, idol worship, stealing, etc. Sin shows up in our everyday behaviors, like: gossip, lying, cheating, pride, jealousy, unrighteous anger, gluttony, greed, and judging people, just to name a few.

The Bible very clearly states that those who do not enjoy a saving relationship with God through Jesus are condemned to a life apart from God for all eternity. Born into the sin of Adam and Eve, we are all sinful by nature. Romans 3:23 states, "For all have sinned and fall short of the glory of God." However, despite our sin, God desires to be in close relationship with every individual He created. How is that possible? God sent His Son, Jesus, to bridge the enormous gap that sin creates between Himself and us.

Although our sin separates us from God, no sin is too big for God to forgive, and we don't have to get our lives in order before coming to Jesus Christ. God loves you just the way you are. Romans 5:8 says, "But God demonstrates His own love for us in this: While we were still sinners, Christ died for us."

God, in His unconditional, infinite love for His creation, established a way we could be forgiven, redeemed, and reconciled to Him. He sent His one and only Son, Jesus Christ, to earth to be the sacrificial Lamb and die on the cross to pay the penalty for our sins. In doing so, He formed a bridge between a sinful people and a perfect God. He provided *the only way* we could experience restored relationship with God, the Father. John 3:16-18 says,

> "For God so loved the world that He gave His one and only Son, that whoever believes in Him shall not perish but have eternal life. For God did not send His Son into the world to condemn the world, but to save the world through Him. Whoever believes in Him is not condemned, but whoever does not believe stands condemned already because he has not believed in the name of God's one and only Son."

God gives us the opportunity to live with Him eternally, through His Son, when we confess Jesus as our Savior and Lord. "For the wages of sin is death, but the gift of God is eternal life in Christ Jesus our Lord" (Romans 6:23). God promises that we will be saved when we accept Jesus' death on the cross as payment for our sin and believe in His resurrection from the dead. Did you hear that? Jesus didn't remain in the grave. He's not dead! Jesus is alive! We can have a relationship with a *living* God through Jesus Christ because He lives! Isn't that the greatest news you've ever heard? Yes!

If you have never confessed your sin and invited Jesus into your heart, what are you waiting for? Simply *believing* in God isn't enough. To reiterate, Jesus Christ is *the only way* to a restored relationship with your heavenly Father. Jesus said, "I am the way and the truth and the life. No one comes to the Father except through Me" (John 14:6). Do you desire to walk with Jesus? Do you want to let Him heal your hurts and fill that hole in your heart that nothing else and no one else can fill? Do you want to accept Jesus Christ as your Savior and Lord today?

There is nothing you can do to earn your own salvation, and no measure of good behavior and good works will get you into heaven. It is by God's free gift of His amazing grace and the death of His Son, Jesus Christ, on the cross that your sins are forgiven, and you are reconciled to God. The way to experience forgiveness of sins and reconciliation with God is to acknowledge that Jesus Christ is the Son of God, accept that He died for your sins, ask His forgiveness, and invite Him to be the Lord of your life. When you do this, God sends His Holy Spirit to live in your heart.

In Revelation 3:20, Jesus says, "Here I am! I stand at the door and knock. If anyone hears My voice and opens the door, I will come in and eat with him, and he with Me." Jesus stands at the door of your heart today and knocks. Do you hear His voice? Will you open the door and invite Him in? If you are not a follower of Christ yet, and your heart's desire is to know and feel God's presence and peace daily, then accept Jesus Christ as your Savior and start your new "relationship" with Him today. You may sense the Holy Spirit of God encouraging you to make a decision for Christ right now. If so, say these words in prayer to God:

> *Dear Heavenly Father,*
>
> *I confess that I have sinned, and I know that my sin separates me from You. Please forgive me for all my sins. I accept that Your Son, Jesus Christ, came to save me by Your grace. He died on the cross to pay the penalty for my sin and provide the only way back to You. God, I believe You raised Jesus from the dead. He is alive and lives to intercede for me.*
>
> *Jesus, I invite You into my heart today to be the Lord of my life and give me a fresh start. Thank You for the promise of eternal life in heaven with You, and for the gift of Your Holy Spirit Whom You send to live in my heart right now. Please help me hear Your voice within me and lead a life that glorifies You. In Jesus' name, I pray. Amen.*

Romans 10:9-10 says, "That if you confess with your mouth, 'Jesus is Lord,' and believe in your heart that God raised Him from the dead, you will be saved. For it is with your heart that you believe and are justified, and it is with your mouth that you confess and are saved." If you prayed this prayer for the first time and were sincere, there is great rejoicing in heaven today! You are forgiven, and you will spend eternity with your heavenly Father. Your fate has been sealed by the Holy Spirit Whom God gave you just now. You are a child of God! Welcome to His family. The Bible says,

> And this is the testimony: God has given us eternal life, and this life is in His Son. He who has the Son has life; he who does not have the Son of God does not have life. I write these things to you who believe in the name of the Son of God so that you may know that you have eternal life. This is the assurance we have in approaching God: that if we ask anything according to His will, He hears us. And if we know that He hears us—whatever we ask—we know that we have what we asked of Him. (1 John 5:11-15)

> Therefore, if anyone is in Christ, he is a new creation; the old has gone, the new has come! (2 Corinthians 5:17)

If you invited Jesus Christ to be your Savior today, you now have a new life in Him, because He lives in you. By the power of God's Holy Spirit within you, your actions and attitudes will change. With His help, you will discard your old way of living and seek to live a life that is more pleasing to God.

Record today's date and your name in the space provided on the next page. This is your spiritual re-birth date. You are born again in Jesus Christ. Happy Birthday! God adopted you as His son or daughter today. This is the first day of the rest of your life!

My Spiritual Birthday

Today, _____/_____/_____, I prayed to receive Jesus Christ as my Savior and Lord.

I, _____, am a child of the King!

Preface

I find it humorous—and necessary to admit to you—that as I started writing this book, I experienced my own roadblock to hearing God's voice regarding the content of this book. Coincidence? Most likely not.

For my first two published books, I can boldly proclaim that God gave me the ideas, including the book and chapter titles, outlines, and words to use. He deserves all the praise and glory for the entirety of both projects. I take no credit for anything. Praise You, Lord!

As a starting point when I put pen to page to create this book, I extracted the seven roadblocks listed in Book One of the **Hearing God's Voice Series,** ***7 Simple Steps to Hearing God's Voice: Listening to God Made Easy***. But then, I relied on myself and my own ideas to generate content. To my regret, that method did not produce much success. Yes, I had thoughts about how it should be laid out.. However, when I sat down to write, no great words or sentences came together.

My usual practice is to offer up a prayer each time I sit down to write, before I ever access the manuscript file in Microsoft Word. I ask God to give me His words and ideas. I humble myself by visualizing me pouring myself out of my body, and I ask the Lord to fill me with the fullness of Christ. I pray for protection from attacks and confusion from the enemy. I ask God to work through the words to touch readers' hearts and get the finished book into the hands of those He wants to reach.

However, somewhere in this project, I (my head) got in the way. I thought it was up to me to produce interesting, substantive content for this book, and that responsibility seemed daunting. Even when I practiced my usual prayer ritual, no significant concepts poured into my brain for the chapter content about the seven roadblocks. I questioned whether I had heard God correctly when I began to break down a larger manuscript into smaller books to include in this series. *Did He give me that idea, or did I come up with that on my own? Is this work ordained by Him, or did I run in my own direction on this project? Did the enemy get involved and give me busy work to keep me from God's perfect plan for my time?* Great questions, right?

So I set down my pen (computer) for a few months, to meditate and pray about this book. Today, as I return to my computer in an attempt to write again, it's obvious to me that God allowed my writer's block to enforce my knowledge and understanding that I am nothing without Him. I am so humbled right now knowing that I cannot do any of this without the power of God's Spirit in me. He permitted me to see and recognize my complete dependence on Him to accomplish the work He gives me to do.

Today, I lay prostrate on the floor humbling myself before God, praying that He will take control of this book. I ask that He pour His Spirit into me with thoughts and words from Him—the message He wants His people to hear. I pray He will hide me and protect me from Satan's attacks of interference, confusion, deceit, and disillusionment.

You see, Satan invests large chunks of time in distracting my attention from the work God calls me to do. The devil whispers in my head, things like:

- ❖ You are not a gifted writer. You have no creative talent.
- ❖ You don't have the authority to write a book like this.
- ❖ Who are you kidding? You can't do this. Aren't you afraid of failing?
- ❖ Why did you commit to writing a book series when you can't find words for this book?
- ❖ You don't have enough to say to write all these books. You can't even write the second book. You'll never get this done.
- ❖ This wasn't God's will. This was your own idea. You might as well quit now.

Have you ever heard discouraging voices in your head that planted similar thoughts? Well, I like to think I am smart enough, and alert enough, to recognize when Satan speaks to me in this manner. However, I still find that I listen to his lies and start to believe them. That crafty villain knows exactly what to say to mess me up and keep me from God's work!

Well, here's my response to my opponent, the devil:

> Get thee behind me, Satan! There is no truth in you. You are a liar and the father of lies (John 8:44). You hold no power over me! I will not permit myself to believe your misconceptions. For God did not give me a spirit of timidity, but a spirit of power, of love and of self-discipline (2 Tim. 1:7).

I worship a risen Savior who has been given power over everything in heaven and on earth and under the earth (Phil. 2:10). He has seated me next to Himself in the heavenly realms (Eph. 2:6) and given me the same power over you (Eph. 1:17-23). Jesus gave me authority to overcome your power (Luke 10:19).

My Lord, Jesus Christ, defeated you once and for all when He went to the cross on my behalf. By the power of Jesus' name and His blood, I claim victory over you for all times, in all places! I can do everything through Him Who gives me strength (Phil. 4:13)! He who began a good work in me will carry it on to completion! (Phil. 1:6)! By the power of the Holy Spirit, Who gives me the wisdom and words of God, I will write this book and all the books in the series. Consider it done!

Now that I have exposed the lies of the deceiver and combatted them with the truth from God's Word, I am set free (John 8:32). Jesus reminded me of the truth and set me free, so I am free indeed (John 8:36). This process can be successful only to the extent that I am alert to the devil's ways, pay attention to the voice of God within me, and claim the truth victoriously in Jesus' name. Isn't that true for all the lies of the enemy? They hold only as much power over us as we allow them to.

It is unusual for me to include my mind battles in my preface. However, in my prayer today, I asked God to confirm the "lie vs. truth" format I had started to lay out in each chapter. This example of the deceiver's mind games confirms the frailty of the human mentality and proves the necessity for this arrangement throughout the book.

You may want to take a similar approach and step up your prayer life as you study this book. Be alert and aware of all the ways the enemy may try to divert, distract, confuse, or delude you as you make your way through this narrative. The devil definitely does not want you to discover his deceiving tactics outlined in the pages that follow. Use God's Word, as I have on the previous page, to rebuke the enemy and take authority over him. He has only as much power as you give to him. As a child of God, you may confidently claim your victory and authority in Jesus' name, and then, stand firm, holding to your faith. Give thanks to the Lord, for He is good!

Lord, You are awesome and magnificent! I praise You for Your goodness. I thank You for the confirmation I needed to keep going in this direction. I thank You for meeting the needs of the reader in this fashion. You are my All in All! I am nothing without You. Be glorified in me, through me, and through this book. I pray this Scripture back to You, God:

> Now to You who are able to do immeasurably more than all I ask or imagine, according to Your power that is at work within me, to You be glory in the church and in Christ Jesus throughout all generations, for ever and ever! Amen. (See Ephesians 3:20)

Introduction

Why don't I hear God's voice? Have you ever wondered why others hear God's voice, but you don't? I admit, this question kept me guessing for many years. In this book, I will share with you seven things that kept me from hearing God speak. Is it possible any or all of these same obstructions block your clear reception of God's voice?

Before you think *But God won't speak to me because...* (Fill in the blank yourself), let me tell you, it's really very simple. If you have accepted Jesus Christ as your Savior and Lord, then God ***does*** speak to you. However, something may be deafening your ears to His voice. This book introduces seven roadblocks that may stand in your way of hearing God speak. As you read on, see if any of these barriers might be keeping you from enjoying two-way conversation and intimate relationship with your Savior and Lord.

After twenty years of following Christ and yet struggling with clinical depression, I was ready to throw in the towel. I could only hope there was more to life than what I'd experienced. I heard believers talk about a relationship with Jesus. I thought I had one. I talked to God, but unfairly, I didn't leave room in the conversation for God to speak to me. I didn't *believe* He would speak to me. *Doubt* was one of the roadblocks standing in my way of hearing God's voice. I didn't consider that the big God of the universe would speak to little ole me.

I couldn't have been more wrong. About fifteen years ago, it all changed for me. One night, while talking to God, I actually made time to listen. I heard a voice in my thoughts that I knew was not my own. It was God! He spoke to *me*, an average girl. Now I know ordinary people hear from God, too. Are you ordinary? Do you question what keeps you from hearing God's voice? If so, this book was written just for you.

You may wonder, *Why doesn't God speak to me? What am I doing wrong? How do I go about hearing His voice?* I wrestled with these same uncertainties. In my quest for answers, God blessed me far beyond my heart's desire. My relationship with the Lord grew stronger and deeper as I learned how to enjoy *two-way* communication with Him.

Does your relationship with Jesus lack the WOW factor? Mine did. But hearing God's voice added an amazing new dimension to my adventure with Jesus Christ. Whenever we listen to God's voice within us, we achieve a greater intimacy with the Lord. Hearing God's voice is one of the keys to a deeper connection with Jesus Christ. It's absolutely life-changing and life-giving!

Are you eager to hear what God is saying to you? Are you ready to consider what might be hampering your ability to hear Him? Are you asking, *What keeps me from hearing God's voice? How do I eliminate these barriers between God and me? Why am I traveling at construction speed in my faith while my friends cruise along at 70 mph?* This book will answer your questions and walk you through a proven process to knocking down the roadblocks that keep you from hearing God. Remove your hurdles, and accelerate your connection with the Holy Spirit who dwells within you. Your search for deeper intimacy with God is about to yield results.

After regularly hearing God speak for the last fifteen years, I nailed down *7 Roadblocks to Hearing God Speak*. The chapters of this book explain seven reasons you may be deaf to the voice of God within you. Practicing any or all of the behaviors identified here may cause you to feel that the all-powerful God will not speak to you because you are not worthy or qualified to hear Him. Truly, despite your flaws and feelings of inadequacy, God continues to pursue you passionately. He doesn't wait until you are perfect and sin-free to speak to you. The Holy Spirit of God communicates with you all day, every day, in many different ways. He's anxiously waiting for you to listen and recognize His voice!

As a Christian, you have the *living* God dwelling inside you, so why wouldn't you be able to hear His voice? Well, these seven things may stand in the way: **doubt, fear, pride, worry, busyness, disobedience, and an unwillingness to forgive**. To be clear, these behaviors won't necessarily keep God from speaking to you, but they may keep you from hearing Him. The indwelling Holy Spirit helps you become more Christ-like, so you have to be able to hear and recognize God's voice within to utilize the promptings and assistance the Holy Spirit offers you in the journey of sanctification.

This book will help you identify and eliminate the seven barriers that may cause deafness to God's voice. Learn how to crush these deterrents and strengthen your relationship with the Lord.

Achieve amazing results when you clear the path to listening to God. Truly, it's worth your time and effort. In fact, it's vital to experiencing the abundant life Jesus Christ came to give you!

Chapter 1

DOUBT

The Enemy of Belief

Immediately Jesus reached out His hand and caught him. "You of little faith," He said, "why did you doubt?" (Matthew 14:31)

Doubt is belief. It's contrary belief to the truth.
—Dr. Ed Smith

From God's Heart to Yours

My child, why do you doubt that I will speak to you? Why don't you believe that you can hear My voice? Do you lack faith? Even if you have only a speck of faith, believe that you will hear Me, and you will have what you yearn for. Do you lack understanding? Let Me set you straight. If you have accepted Jesus Christ as your Savior and Lord, you already have everything you need to hear My voice. I am with you at all times. I live in your heart, and I have given you the mind of Christ. You know My voice. Simply be still and listen.

My Spirit within you communicates My thoughts to you. Do not pay attention to the other voices in your head. They will only confuse you and mislead you. But My Spirit will guide you down the paths I have laid out for you. He gives you My wisdom and encouragement. He speaks only the truth and does not depart from My Word. He reminds you what I have said and interprets Scripture for you. He prays on your behalf when you know not what to pray.

Beloved one, I desire to speak with you daily—even throughout your day. Please seek Me in the morning to start your day out right. Talk to Me before you get out of bed. Speak to me again at breakfast. Take Me with you to the gym and to the office. Communicate with Me while you drive your car. Seek Me before those important meetings and conversations. I show up at all your practices and sporting events. I am present with you in your classes. I sit with you while you eat lunch and dinner. Please think of Me more often. I am with you at all times. I will never leave you or forget you. Please do not forget Me or pretend you do not hear Me.

I am your shepherd, and you are my sheep. My sheep know My voice, and they listen to Me. Get up a little early tomorrow morning and meet with Me alone, away from all distractions. I long to communicate My thoughts to you. I have so much to say. Will you make time for Me, dear friend?

DOUBT

Inexperience and ignorance kept me in a bubble for the first two decades of my Christian walk. After I accepted Jesus Christ as my Savior and invited Him into my heart at the age of eighteen, I lived a good Christian life, doing all the right things. I began a Bible study in the book of John. I continued to attend my childhood church, where I was involved in a young adult group. I prayed and read my Bible regularly. I listened to Christian music and read inspirational books. I tried not to sin too often, but when I did, I asked God's forgiveness as soon as I felt convicted.

Over the years, I heard other believers, like pastors, talk about hearing God's voice, but I never considered that God would speak to me. Often, I heard Christ followers say that their faith was more of a relationship than a religion. I thought that praying to God and reading His Word meant I had a relationship with Him. However, I never left room in my prayers—conversations with God—for Him to speak His mind. I never even attempted to listen to His voice, because I *didn't believe* He would speak to me. I occasionally sensed God speaking to me through Scripture but never even dreamed He would speak to me in my thoughts.

Sound familiar? Can you relate to any part of this story? If so, keep reading.

At nineteen, I landed a great full-time office position at a pharmaceutical plant, and I married the love of my life at the age of twenty. My first child was born after I turned twenty-six, and my second child came along two years later. After my firstborn, I transitioned to part-time office work at the wholesale greenhouse operation that employed my husband. I continued to work part-time most of the year and full-time during the busy season, March through May. As my children grew, I served in their school classrooms and took on leadership roles in church activities. I had a full, busy life that left me no time to spend alone with God to nurture my relationship with Him. Ironically, the more time I put into serving my family, my job, my church, and my other commitments, the more lonely and unappreciated I felt.

Looking back, I see that I fit the description of the lukewarm Christian. I wasn't cold toward God, but I wasn't on fire for Him either. I enjoyed a "normal" life, which resembled the lives of many other Christians I knew. And after twenty years of this blissful monotony, I wondered if this was all there was to life. If so, I wasn't sure I wanted to go on living.

While I was in counseling for clinical depression, my psychologist shared his recent boost in his walk with the Lord. He had learned how to listen to God's voice. I could see the new passion and excitement he had for Jesus. It sparked my interest in knowing Jesus more intimately. My counselor encouraged me to spend time alone with God: to talk to God and then listen to Him, writing down what I heard Him say. Unfamiliar with this practice, I made many attempts over many weeks before I realized success. ***7 Simple Steps to Hearing God's Voice***. the first book in the ***Hearing God's Voice Series***, walks you through my process of learning how to hear and recognize when God speaks.

I soon realized that the obstacle of ***doubt*** had prevented me from hearing God's voice for all those years. My skepticism profoundly contributed to my deafness toward God's voice. Actually, it kept me from *attempting* to listen to God at all. I lacked faith that God would speak to me; therefore, I heard nothing.

Hebrews 11:1 says, "Now faith is being sure of what we hope for and certain of what we do not see." We might add to that: It's being certain of what we do not hear. To hear God's voice, we must be certain we will hear it! Do a faith check. Examine your own heart and mind. Do you believe that God will speak to you? Do you understand that God speaks to you through His Holy Spirit, Who lives in you? You can believe it, because Jesus said it in John 16:13-15:

> "But when He, the Spirit of truth, comes, *He will guide you* into all truth. He will not speak on His own; *He will speak* only what He hears, and *He will tell you* what is yet to come. He will bring glory to Me by taking from what is Mine and *making it known to you*. All that belongs to the Father is Mine. That is why I said the Spirit will take from what is Mine and *make it known to you.*" (Emphasis mine)

Not understanding the role of the Holy Spirit kept me from leaving room in my prayer time for God to speak. I prayed, but I didn't stop talking long enough to listen. I didn't believe I would hear God speak to me because I didn't understand that He spoke through the Holy Spirit. But when I started delving into Scripture and reading inspirational books about the Holy Spirit, my appreciation grew for all that He does for me. A more thorough knowledge of the third person in the Holy Trinity afforded me a better understanding, which led to an increased trust that enabled me to hear His verbal communications in my thoughts.

Remember the story of Jesus walking on the water from Matthew 14:22-33? Jesus made the disciples get into the boat and go ahead of Him to the other side of the lake. Then He went into the hills alone to pray. When evening came and He returned from the hills, the boat was already in the middle of the lake. So He walked on the lake's surface toward the boat. The disciples were terrified, thinking Jesus was a ghost. But Jesus said to them, "Take courage! It is I. Don't be afraid."

"Lord, if it's you," Peter replied, "tell me to come to you on the water."

"Come," He said.

Peter stepped out of the boat and walked on the water to Jesus. But when he saw the wind, he began to sink in fear, crying out, "Lord, save me!"

Jesus reached out His hand and caught Peter. He asked Peter, "You of little faith, why did you doubt?"

Notice that Peter *did* walk on the water. He trusted Jesus enough to get out of the boat, but when the wind came up, his faith took a downward turn. He lost his confidence in Christ and doubted His power to keep him on top of the water. Peter's doubt put constraints on what Jesus would do for him. This lesson teaches us to be certain that God gives us the power to do what He calls us to do. Jesus would not have called Peter out of the boat to let him drown in the lake. Rather, He invited Peter to believe in His ability to empower him to do the impossible.

Similarly, when I doubted that God would speak to me, I put constraints on what God would do for me. My doubt put up a roadblock between God and me. Uncertainty erected an obstruction in my two-way communication with the Lord. Notice I didn't say that my doubt *limited* what God could do. More precisely, my hesitation hindered my own ability to hear my heavenly Father. It wasn't until I entertained the possibility that God would speak to me that the ears of my heart were opened to hear His voice.

Also observe that Jesus reached out His hand to His friend when Peter's doubt sprang up. Jesus does not let us perish in our lack of faith and trust. He continues to pursue us and use our trials to 1) make us more dependent on Him, 2) bring us closer to Him, 3) increase our trust in His power, and 4) mature us in our faith. He holds our hand until our trust in His power catches up.

Hebrews 3:7-12 offers a warning against unbelief:

> So, as the Holy Spirit says: "Today, if you hear His voice, do not harden your hearts as you did in the rebellion, during the time of testing in the desert, where your fathers tested and tried Me and for forty years saw what I did. That is why I was angry with that generation, and I said, 'Their hearts are always going astray, and they have not known My ways.' So I declared on oath in My anger, 'They shall never enter My rest.'"
> See to it, brothers, that none of you has a sinful, unbelieving heart that turns away from the living God.

As it did with Peter, doubt causes us to lose our footing as believers and sink in our lack of faith in Jesus. It makes us dependent on ourselves, not trusting in the power of God in us. We must remember that we have the Spirit of the living, Almighty God dwelling in us. He gives us the faith to believe and empowers us to do all that He prepares and plans for us to do. Romans 8:11 says, "And if the Spirit of Him who raised Jesus from the dead is living in you, He who raised Christ from the dead will also give life to your mortal bodies through His Spirit, Who lives in you." We have the same strength, ability, and authority residing in us that raised Jesus Christ from the dead. Pretty amazing, right? All we have to do is recognize that fact, own it, and call on that power of God in us. Praise the Lord that He sent a member of the Holy Trinity to enable us to accomplish all that He has prepared in advance for us to achieve!

We must ask ourselves, what causes the doubt in the first place? If you read my note in the **Preface**, you will gain insight into one answer to that question: Satan speaks to our hearts with lies and stirs our spirits to question God's power and our own abilities.

To consider what doubt really portrays is disconcerting. When I don't believe that God will speak to me, I really make the following false assumptions and statements about God:

- ❖ He doesn't have the desire to speak to me.
- ❖ He doesn't have the ability to speak to me.
- ❖ He isn't true to His promise in Scripture that He will speak to me.
- ❖ His power is limited.
- ❖ Jesus' death on the cross was not enough to reconcile me to God.
- ❖ He doesn't care about me.

Do you sense the selfishness in these accusations? I just made it all about myself, not about God's design and desire for His children. Moreover, I grossly reduced the awesome power of the death and resurrection of Jesus Christ. I disowned my identity in Jesus, and I disclaimed my heavenly inheritance. Do you ever have any of the thoughts and feelings I listed above? Do you see how that could create a barrier between you and God? How it may cause God to limit His communication with you?

Doubt is the enemy of belief in the truth, as James 1:5-8 says:

> If any of you lacks wisdom, he should ask God, Who gives generously to all without finding fault, and it

will be given to him. But when he asks, he must believe and not doubt, because he who doubts is like a wave of the sea, blown and tossed by the wind. That man should not think He will receive anything from the Lord; he is a double-minded man, unstable in all he does.

Dr. Ed Smith, founder of Transformation Prayer Ministry, says, "Doubt is belief—it's contrary belief to the truth…You believe something else." Dr. Smith suggests that we can have simultaneous, contradictory beliefs, holding a lie and the truth at the same time—making us a double-minded, unstable people. (See his full message on James 1:2-8 on his website, www.transformationprayer.org.) We must ask God for His wisdom and listen to His voice, but we must ask in faith, without doubt. God *is* speaking to us. He wants us to know what to do, but it's possible that we can't hear Him because we are entertaining a lie and a truth at the same time.

Dr. Smith gives the example that a certain man believes that God will provide for all his needs. Then the man loses his job, so he becomes worried and full of anxiety. He believes God will provide, and yet now he fears that without a job his needs may not be met. Back and forth. Back and forth. Double-minded. That man is like a wave of the sea, blown and tossed by the wind, unstable in what he believes. His doubts might prevent him from hearing God's voice during his hardships.

When we doubt God's promises, power, and abilities, we give a whole lot of undeserved power to the devil, who sows the seed of skepticism in our minds. In each of the seven roadblock chapters, we will examine three lies that Satan instills in our minds with regard to each encumbrance. Of course, these lies are not the only falsehoods he implants. They represent a sampling to get you thinking about the possible causes of your misgivings. Then, following Jesus' example of battling Satan with God's Word when the devil tempted Him in the desert, we will dispel each lie with the truth from Scripture.

    As long as we accept, believe, and/or invest in Satan's lies, he is happy because we remain in bondage to him. To break free from the strongholds of the devil, we must recognize the lies and overcome them with the truth of God's Word. When you find your mind bombarded with the fabricated claims of the father of lies, replace the devil's deceit with the indisputable truth of Scripture. Wash away the dishonest dirt. Rehearse and repeat the truths of Scripture.

    Some falsehoods swirling around in our heads evolve from the idea that God does not still speak to His people today, except to a select few spiritually mature figures, and if we do hear God speak, we can't be sure it's actually His voice. Are these lies feeding your doubt?

LIE #1: God does *not* still speak today.

Do you believe God still speaks? So often, we minimize the desires of God and His power at work today. We rationalize that God and Jesus performed miracles in Bible times but do not operate in the same way now. Hebrews 13:8 says, "Jesus Christ is the same yesterday and today and forever." What part of that verse implies that if God spoke directly to people in the Old Testament and Jesus spoke directly to people in the New Testament, He will not speak directly to His people today? Thankfully, none of it.

God gave us His Word so that we would understand His desires, His character, and His power in our lives, enabling us to live in a Christ-like manner that is pleasing and glorifying to Him. The Bible is not an outdated book. Rather it is a rock-solid, Spirit-breathed, unwavering "how-to" manual on living a Spirit-filled, abundant life in the power of the Holy Spirit that dwells within every Christ follower. The fact that God sends the Holy Spirit to make our hearts His home indicates that He is alive and active in every moment of our existence today.

God *does* still speak today. When we ask Him in faith, without any doubt, to provide His wisdom, He will impart it to us in generous amounts, usually through the voice of His Holy Spirit and through His Word. When we are stable in our faith and not held in bondage by believing lies, we will hear Him clearly.

TRUTH #1: God's Holy Spirit, who dwells in the heart of every believer, speaks what He hears from God.

When Jesus appeared to His disciples after His resurrection, He instructed them to wait to receive the gift of the Holy Spirit before they began spreading the news of the gospel (see Acts 1:4-5). Fortunately, Christ followers today do not have to wait for the arrival of the Holy Spirit. The moment we accept Jesus as our Savior and Lord, we receive the gift of the Holy Spirit—no waiting required. From day one of our spiritual rebirth, we enjoy the gift of the living God dwelling in us, speaking to us, making the things of God known to us. We simply have to listen to His still, small voice within and learn to recognize when He speaks to us. In addition, we need to be in tune to the many different ways He speaks to us from external sources, including the Bible, other people, the words of a Christian song or book, the ideas He places in our thoughts, and our dreams and visions.

I regret to admit that it's much too easy for me to forget that God's Holy Spirit dwells in me and to go about living my life as if He isn't there. Too often, I go off in my own direction without consulting the Holy Spirit before making decisions and plans. My plans might be good, but God's plans for me are always better. Do you ever find that you do things without checking in with God first?

In Joshua 1:5, God promises He will never leave us or forget us. Why is it that we so quickly forget Him and His presence in our hearts? It takes a daily, moment-by-moment, conscious effort to pay close attention to the voice of the Holy Spirit as He directs our thoughts, our tongue, our actions, our reactions, and our steps according to His will.

Giving God first place in all areas of our existence requires perpetual practice. It's unnatural. It goes against our selfish, sinful flesh. We want to run ahead and design our own blueprints for life, living the way we desire, when God has already designed a more excellent way for us. His perfect plans are to prosper us, give us hope and a future (see Jeremiah 29:11). He knows all things, especially what is best for us. If we just make time to listen to God, He'll let us in on His plans for our lives. Only when we live according to His desires and plans will we experience His peace and joy in abundance, the way He intended.

The Truth in God's Word:

"But when He, the Spirit of truth, comes, *He will guide you* into all truth. He will not speak on His own; *He will speak* only what He hears, and *He will tell you* what is yet to come. He will bring glory to Me by taking from what is Mine and *making it known to you*. All that belongs to the Father is Mine. That is why I said the Spirit will take from what is Mine and *make it known to you*." (John 16:13-15; emphasis mine)

"For I know the plans I have for you," declares the Lord, "plans to prosper you and not to harm you, plans to give you hope and a future. Then you will call upon Me and come and pray to Me and I will listen to you. You will seek Me and find Me when you seek Me with all your heart." (Jeremiah 29:11-13)

LIE #2: God speaks only to prophets, pastors, and spiritual leaders.

Before getting to know God better and more fully understanding the role of the Holy Spirit, I believed He would never have the desire or take the time to speak to someone as lowly as I am. Listening to pastors and church leaders speak about hearing from God and receiving verbal direction from Him was believable, but not often did I hear lay people speak about it. Maybe I wasn't paying attention, didn't hang with the right crowd, or just completely excused the possibility from my mind.

Yes, God speaks to prophets, pastors, spiritual leaders, AND ordinary people. God longs for a close relationship and open communication with each and every one of His children. If you are a Christ follower, God speaks to Y-O-U. Let's look at some of the average people God spoke to in the Old Testament:

Adam and Eve

From the very beginning of time, God desired personal intimacy with His creation through two-way conversation. Genesis 3 describes God walking in the Garden of Eden and speaking to Adam and Eve, the first man and woman He created. God verbally communicated with them before they sinned, and He continued to speak with them after they disobeyed His instructions. God also spoke to Cain and Abel, the sons of Adam and Eve. The Bible makes no mention that Adam and Eve were pastors or prophets, and since they were the first humans He created and no one else existed, it is safe to say they were not spiritual leaders outside their home.

Noah

Genesis 5 and 6 do not say much about Noah before God called him to construct the ark, other than that he found favor in the eyes of the Lord, he was a righteous man, and he walked with God. The Lord was fond of Noah because he led an upright, honorable life in the midst of people whose hearts and tendencies were only evil all the time. However, Noah was an ordinary man. Scripture does not say he held a position of pastor or was a prophet or spiritual leader when God chose to speak to him. Yet God used him to build the ark that would save his family and the animals from a life-destroying flood.

Abram (Abraham)

In Genesis 12:1-3, the Lord spoke directly to Abram, another ordinary man who would become the father of many nations. God made a covenant with him that his offspring would be as numerous as the stars in the night sky. Abram was seventy-five years old when God first instructed him to leave his father's house and go to the land God would show him. No mention of his character included any spiritual leadership qualities before this time.

Moses

In Exodus 3:4-6, God first appeared to Moses and spoke to him from within a burning bush. Read part of their conversation below.

God: Moses, Moses!

Moses: Here I am.

God: Do not come any closer. Take off your sandals, for the place where you are standing is holy ground. I am the God of your father, the God of Abraham, the God of Isaac and the God of Jacob.

Moses was an average man; however, God spoke directly to him. He told Moses that He was sending him to bring the Israelites out of Egypt. Moses resisted the call of God and did not quickly submit himself to God's will. He argued and reasoned with God.

Still, his initial reluctance to obey God's call did not keep God from pursuing Moses to be His chosen leader.

Joshua

After Moses led the Israelites out of Egypt through the desert toward the promised land, God replaced Moses with Joshua. He would escort God's chosen people on the final steps of their long journey into the land they would inherit. Joshua did not already hold a position of leadership when God spoke to him the first time (at least the first time that's recorded in Scripture). When He commissioned him as the new leader, God gave Joshua one of the most instructive, encouraging, and promising Scripture passages that we still lean on today:

> "No one will be able to stand up against you all the days of your life. As I was with Moses, so I will be with you; *I will never leave you or forsake you.* Be strong and courageous, because you will lead these people to inherit the land I swore to their forefathers to give them. Be strong and very courageous. Be careful to obey all the law My servant Moses gave you; do not turn from it to the right or to the left, that you may be successful wherever you go. Do not let this Book of the Law depart from your mouth; meditate on it day and night, so that you may be careful to do everything written in it. Then you will be prosperous and successful. Have I not commanded you? Be strong and courageous. Do not be terrified; do not be discouraged, for *the Lord your God will be*

with you wherever you go." (Joshua 1:5-9; emphasis mine)

Samuel

During Eli's priesthood, the people of Israel rarely heard God's voice. From the time Samuel was a very young boy, he served in the temple under Eli (see 1 Samuel 3). He did not yet know the Lord: The word of the Lord had not yet been revealed to him. One evening, as Samuel was lying in the Lord's temple, where the ark of God was, the Lord called him. Samuel was just a preadolescent boy. He grew to be a prophet of God; however, God began speaking to Samuel at a very early age—no Master of Divinity degree or leadership skills were required.

David

Young David, son of Jesse, was just seventeen when the Spirit of the Lord came upon him in power. Acts 13:22 says that God called David "a man after My own heart". Even though David committed many sins, God loved David because he sought His will, and he did what the Lord commanded him. David remained humble, he depended on God, he maintained a relationship with God, and he worshiped God with reckless abandon. David, too, was just an average shepherd boy when God first spoke to him.

I've spotlighted some of the more prominent figures in the Bible for a reason. God spoke to them when they were unknowns. They had no special degrees or spiritual leadership skills that we know of when God first chose to speak to them. Of course God speaks to prophets, pastors, and spiritual leaders. But God speaks to average, ordinary Christ followers, too.

Through reading the New Testament, we know Jesus, Who is God in the flesh, walked the earth as a man and spoke to people face to face. Jesus communicated directly with His family, disciples, friends, religious leaders, lepers, sinners, adulterers, and even demons as He drove them out of people. No official title or position was required back then, nor is it required now, to participate in daily two-way communication with the King of kings and Lord of lords. Today we talk to God through prayer, and He speaks to us through the Holy Spirit within us and through His Word.

TRUTH #2: If you are a child of God, you can hear Him speak.

Repetition from a previous section is necessary here. In fact, this verse really answers ***any and all*** claims that you cannot possibly hear God's voice.

> "But when He, the Spirit of truth, comes, *He will guide you* into all truth. He will not speak on His own; *He will speak* only what He hears, and *He will tell*

you what is yet to come. He will bring glory to Me by taking from what is Mine and *making it known to you.* All that belongs to the Father is Mine. That is why I said the Spirit will take from what is Mine and *make it known to you.*" (John 16:13-15; emphasis mine)

In John 14:16, Jesus Himself promises that the Father will give you another Counselor—the Spirit of Truth—Who will be with you forever. He continues that you will know the Spirit because He lives with you and is in you. Furthermore, in John 14:20, Jesus says that He is in the Father, you are in Him, and He is in you. Since Jesus and the Holy Spirit are in you, there is no reason you should not hear His voice within you if you are paying close attention, poised to listen, and not putting up any of the seven roadblocks discussed in this book.

God gave you the Holy Spirit to seal you as His child until the day of redemption. The Spirit helps you live a more Christ-like life, which brings God glory. God knew that you could not accomplish this on your own, that you needed the Helper. The Spirit of God dwells in you, counsels you, encourages you, convicts you of sin, helps you understand God's Word, reminds you of the truth in Scripture, and gives you the faith to trust in God and His provision. We are truly blessed to receive such an awesome gift from God!

The Truth in God's Word:

He who belongs to God hears what God says. (John 8:47)

#3: I don't know if it's God's voice I hear.

I overhear many believers say they perceive a voice in their thoughts, but they aren't sure it's God's. While it's true that we may hear more than one voice in our heads, that does not give us permission to completely dismiss or ignore the idea that we do hear God speak. It's the listener's responsibility to distinguish the voice of God from the voices of Satan and others. If you have not yet fine-tuned your ear to the channel that God broadcasts from, you may not even realize you *can* hear His voice. Knowing the character of God more fully and understanding how He communicates with His children will afford you a new success in discerning the voices that speak to your heart and mind.

TRUTH #3: The Lord is the good Shepherd, and you are His sheep. His sheep follow Him because they know His voice.

In the narrative in John 10:1-5, Jesus tells the metaphorical story of "The Shepherd and His Flock":

> "I tell you the truth, the man who does not enter the sheep pen by the gate, but climbs in by some other way, is a thief and a robber. The Man who enters by the gate is the Shepherd of His sheep. The watchman opens the gate for Him, and the *sheep listen to His voice*. He calls His own sheep by name and leads them out. When He has brought out all His own, He goes on ahead of them, and His sheep follow Him because *they know His voice*. But they will never follow a stranger; in fact, they will run away from him because they do not recognize a stranger's voice." (Emphasis mine with italicized phrases, and capitalized nouns and pronouns that reference God.)

Then, because the Jews did not understand what He was telling them, Jesus interpreted the story for them in John 10:7-15:

> Therefore Jesus said again, "I tell you the truth, I am the Gate for the sheep. All who ever came before Me were thieves and robbers, but the sheep did not listen to them. I am the Gate; whoever enters through Me will be saved. He will come in and go out, and find pasture. The thief comes only to steal and kill and destroy; I have come that they may have life, and have it to the full.
>
> "I am the good Shepherd. The good Shepherd lays down His life for the sheep. The hired hand is

not the shepherd who owns the sheep. So when he sees the wolf coming, he abandons the sheep and runs away. Then the wolf attacks the flock and scatters it. The man runs away because he is a hired hand and cares nothing for the sheep.

"I am the good Shepherd; I know My sheep and My sheep know Me—just as the Father knows Me and I know the Father—and I lay down My life for the sheep." (Emphasis mine with capitalized nouns and pronouns that reference God.)

In the first half of the story, Jesus relayed that His followers, God's children, listen to His voice, know and recognize His voice, and follow Him. To know and recognize someone's voice, we must spend a lot of time with that person, learning his character and his heart. It's no different with God. The best way to learn more about God is to immerse yourself in the Bible, studying the way He speaks in His Word. Listen to His voice in Scripture—what His words sound like—so you will be equipped to identify His voice when He speaks in your thoughts.

God's words are usually very loving and gentle, while at the same time exuding strength and firmness. They are convicting, not condemning. He speaks with expressions of endearment and encouragement, comfort and compassion. Scripture verses are sprinkled throughout His messages, instructions, and wisdom. His words produce immeasurable peace within. Sometimes His whispers hold sympathy and healing. His truth sets us free from spiritual strongholds. His words are always true and always align with His

Word and His character in the Bible. Often God's words motivate us and stir us into action to carry out His will.

Don't be afraid to ask God for more clarification. Ask Him to confirm that what you just heard came from Him. He may say it to you again and verify it for you. Or you may need to seek confirmation in the Bible or from a trusted friend. God may confirm His whispers through a sermon your pastor preaches, the words of a song on Christian radio, or in a Christian book you are reading. Be sure to check it out further. As many times as you ask for more confirmation, our patient God authenticates what He speaks to you.

On the next page, I have included the same table of my favorite characteristics of God that appears in the first book of this series. I encourage you to open God's Word yourself, and let Him show you His character. Discover what you love most about God.

Jesus said the sheep do not recognize the stranger's voice, and they run from him. Satan is portrayed in the story as the thief, the wolf, and the stranger. It is vital that we are alert to the devil's character and ways in order to discern his voice and workings of deceit in our hearts and minds. Here are more tables from *7 Simple Steps to Hearing God's Voice*. They depict some of Satan's characteristics and methods. Next time you find yourself questioning whether you hear God's voice or not, write down what you hear and weigh it against the characters of God and Satan that you find in the Bible and in the tables that follow.

Know God's Character

Compassionate, gracious, slow to anger, abounding in love and faithfulness	Exodus 34:6
Forgives wickedness, rebellion, and sin	Exodus 34:7
Immanuel – God with us	Matthew 1:23
Everlasting God, Creator, does not grow tired or weary	Isaiah 40:28
The way, the truth, the life	John 14:6
Good Shepherd	John 10:14
Father, Son, and Holy Spirit	Galatians 4:6
Alpha and Omega, First and Last, Beginning and End	Revelation 22:13
Light of the world	John 8:12
Rock, Fortress, Deliverer, Shield, Stronghold, Refuge, Savior	2 Samuel 22:2-3
Wonderful Counselor, Mighty God, Everlasting Father, Prince of Peace	Isaiah 9:6
God is Love; He lives in us	1 John 4:16, Galatians 4:6
Counselor, Spirit of truth	John 14:16-17
Healer, Restorer, Guide	Psalm 147:3, Psalm 23:3
Never leaves us or forgets us	Joshua 1:5

Know the Character and Ways of Satan

He is a roaring lion, looking for someone to devour	1 Peter 5:8-9
Murderer, liar, father of lies	John 8:44
The devil tempts us	Matthew 4:1
He speaks to us and uses Scripture to deceive us	Matthew 4:5-7
Satan masquerades as an angel of light and his servants masquerade as servants of righteousness	2 Corinthians 11:14-15
Messengers of Satan are sent as thorns in the flesh to torment us	2 Corinthians 12:7
He sows evil in the world	Matthew 13:36-39
He takes away the word that was sown in us	Mark 4:15
He prompts our spirits to sin and commit evil	John 13:2
Anger not dealt with gives the devil a foothold	Ephesians 4:26-27
He traps us and holds us captive to do his will	2 Timothy 2:24-26
He is the deceiver, the antichrist	2 John 7
He possesses people with demons and evil spirits	Luke 4:33
Satan entered Judas Iscariot to betray Jesus	Luke 22:3
He asks to sift us like wheat	Luke 22:31-32
Satan fell like lightning from heaven	Luke 10:18
He holds us in slavery by our fear of death	Hebrews 2:15
He has been sinning from the beginning	1 John 3:8
Satan and his angels lost their place in heaven	Revelation 12:8
The great dragon, ancient serpent called the devil or Satan, who leads the world astray	Revelation 12:9
The accuser	Revelation 12:10
Satan is filled with fury	Revelation 12:12
He pursues women	Revelation 12:13
The devil wages war against us	Revelation 12:17
The devil schemes against us	Ephesians 6:11
He is the ruler, authority, power of this dark world, spiritual force of evil in the heavenly realms	Ephesians 6:12
The evil one attacks us with flaming arrows	Ephesians 6:16

Once you are familiar with God's character vs. Satan's character, then you may be able to match the voice in your head against the characteristics you know. Your gut may help you distinguish the source of the whispers in your heart and mind. When you are not at peace, the communication may not be from God. When the words you hear cause you hurt, confusion, doubt, or anxiety, it could mean you are entertaining the lies of the deceiver. Use these two tables in your discernment.

Discern What You Hear

God's Voice	Satan's Voice
Loving	Unloving
Sincere	Conniving
Encouraging	Disapproving
Peaceful	Disturbing
Comforting	Disrupting
Healing	Wounding
Truthful	Deceitful, Lying
Clear, Precise	Confusing
Motivating	Provoking
Aligns with Scripture	Uses Scripture to Deceive
Uplifting	Condescending
Commending	Accusing
Positive	Negative
Forthright	Manipulative
Purifying	Clouding
Refining	Distorting
Gentle	Harsh
Strong, Firm	Indecisive
Redeeming	Shaming
Convicting	Condemning

Discern Who You Hear

God	Satan
Stills you	Rushes you
Reassures you	Frightens you
Leads you	Pushes you
Enlightens you	Confuses you
Forgives you	Condemns you
Calms you	Stresses you
Encourages you	Discourages you
Comforts you	Worries you
Inspires you	Deters you
Frees you	Traps you
Uplifts you	Degrades you
Adores you	Mocks you
Loves you	Hates you
Redeems you	Shames you

The Truth in God's Word:

"The Man who enters by the gate is the shepherd of His sheep. The watchman opens the gate for Him, and *the sheep listen to His voice.* He calls His own sheep by name and leads them out. When He has brought out all His own, He goes on ahead of them, and *His sheep follow Him because they know His voice.*" (John 10:2-4; emphasis mine with italicized phrases and capitalized nouns and pronouns that reference God.)

"I am the good Shepherd; I know My sheep and My sheep know Me—just as the Father knows Me and I know the Father—and I lay down My life for the sheep." (John 10:14-15, emphasis mine with capitalized nouns and pronouns that reference God.)

"My sheep listen to My voice; I know them, and they follow Me." (John 10:27)

"The thief comes only to steal and kill and destroy; I have come that they may have life, and have it to the full." (John 10:10)

Be self–controlled and alert. Your enemy the devil prowls around like a roaring lion looking for someone to devour. Resist him, standing firm in the faith, because you know that your brothers throughout the world are undergoing the same kind of sufferings. (1 Peter 5:8-9)

✝

Near the end of each of these seven chapters, I am excited to share with you excerpts from my devotional book, ***Manna for Today: Bread from Heaven for Each Day***. Written in the voice of God, these excerpts provide examples of how His voice sounds to me, as well as the words of wisdom He spoke to me regarding each of these seven roadblocks, years before this book appeared on my horizon. I hope these entries will inspire and encourage you to remove the barriers and clear the path to intimate two-way conversation between you and God.

"'If you can'?" said Jesus. "Everything is possible for him who believes." Immediately the boy's father exclaimed, "I do believe; help me overcome my unbelief!" (Mark 9:23-24)

Overcome Your Unbelief[1]

My beloved one, I understand your lack of trust. Trust is a virtue of great value. You have been let down so many times by the ones you love. I do not ask you to put your trust in someone that will most certainly disappoint you. I ask you to put your trust in Me, the God of the universe. Have confidence that I will keep My promises to you. I will not fail you. I will not abandon you. I will not disappoint you. I am trustworthy.

I am the truth. You may believe everything that comes from My mouth. I know you want to believe Me and trust Me in your heart. It is your head that stands in your way. You hold on to the disappointment you have known. You cling to the idea that you may rely on no one else. You have had to look after yourself all your life. Stop! I am here. I have been here all the time. You can put your hope and trust in Me. I will keep you safe; I will protect you.

Look into each of the memories you hold on to. Do you see Me? Look more closely. I am there. I have been with you the entire time. You did not see Me, because you did not believe in Me. Now that you know Me, do you see Me? I have walked with you through the fire. I have sheltered you from the storms. I do not let destruction take you over. I have protected you from your enemies.

Consider what I have done for you. I willingly laid down My life for you. If you were the only person on the earth, I still would have died for your sake. Does just anyone do that? No. I am the Lord your God, and you are Mine. When you take the time to know Me better, you will see Me, and your faith will increase. Until then, accept what I say is true. Everything is possible when you believe. I know you want to believe. I will help you overcome your unbelief.

✝

---

[1] Sindy Nagel, "Overcome Your Unbelief" in *Manna for Today: Bread from Heaven for Each Day* (Bloomington, IN: WestBow Press 2012), 91.

"But when He, the Spirit of truth, comes, He will guide you into all truth. He will not speak on His own; He will speak only what He hears, and He will tell you what is yet to come. He will bring glory to Me by taking from what is Mine and making it known to you. All that belongs to the Father is Mine. That is why I said the Spirit will take from what is Mine and make it known to you" (John 16:13-15).

The Holy Trinity[2]

My precious child, I am the awesome triune God. It must be difficult for you to understand, but I AM. I am your Father in heaven. I knew you before I knit you together in your mother's womb. I am the Father of all creation. I am the master of the universe. All things exist because I ordered them into existence. I am the first person of the Trinity. I am the Most High God. I am the author and perfecter of all things seen and unseen. I am the Holy God Almighty. I am God, the Father.

My Son, Jesus Christ, is the Word. He was with Me in the beginning. My Son and I are one. If you know My Son, you know Me. If you have seen My Son, you have seen Me. I sent My Son to save the world. He left His throne in heaven and became flesh. He was offered up as a sacrifice, the Lamb of God, to be the atonement for your sins. He has paid your ransom and bridged the distance that existed between you and Me because of your sin.

My Son is the light of the world. He is the only way to Me, God the Father. Jesus Christ is your eternal high priest. He pleads your case to Me day and night. He has died to give you access to Me, the holy of holies. You may approach My throne without fear and trembling because of the work of My Son. He is the propitiation for your sins. You have regained My favor because of His atoning sacrifice on the cross. Jesus has conquered death and the grave. He is the firstborn from the dead, and He returned to His throne in heaven on My right hand. Jesus Christ, My Son, is the second person in the Holy Trinity.

My Holy Spirit takes up residency in you and lives in your heart, when you confess Jesus as Lord, and believe that God raised Him from the dead. The

---

[2] Sindy Nagel, "The Holy Trinity" in *Manna for Today: Bread from Heaven for Each Day* (Bloomington, IN: WestBow Press 2012), 127.

Holy Spirit is the third person in the Holy Trinity. Jesus sent the Holy Spirit to you, from Me, to guide you into all truth. The Spirit takes what is Mine and makes it known to you. My Holy Spirit, your Counselor, speaks only what He hears from God the Father and God the Son. All that belongs to Me will be made known to you through My Spirit.

My Spirit is My gift to you in Jesus' name. You have access to Me 24/7 through My Spirit who lives in you. I know and see all things with the help of the Holy Spirit. You receive power through the Holy Spirit. You receive good gifts through the Spirit as He determines. Your body is the temple of God whose Spirit lives in you. The Spirit convicts the world of guilt in regard to sin and righteousness and judgment. The Spirit helps you in your weakness. He intercedes for you in accordance with My will. The Spirit, whom I put in your heart, is a deposit guaranteeing your inheritance of eternal life with Me. We are the great three-in-one God. We are God the Father, God the Son, and God the Holy Spirit. We are the Holy Trinity. I AM. Everything I have is available to you. My wisdom and My power I will share with you, by My Spirit, when you ask for it. My protection and My counsel are yours, by My Spirit, when you belong to Me. Everything that Jesus taught on earth will be repeated to you by My Spirit. My healing, My comfort, and My peace are accessible by My Spirit, in Jesus' name. Forgiveness is freely given by Me upon your asking. Knowledge and discernment I offer to you. A life of abundance is yours to receive when you live in Me and walk by My Spirit.

You have no idea of the power, strength, and authority that is available to you by My Spirit Who lives in your heart. Tap into this power by asking Me. Allow My Spirit to guide your steps. Consult with the Spirit on all you do and say. Live in tune with My Spirit. Walk in His ways, and you walk with Me. Live not by might, nor by power, but by My Spirit.

✝

"Blessed is she who has believed that what the Lord has said to her will be accomplished!" (Luke 1:45)

Believe Me[3]

Do you find it difficult to believe what I say? What causes you to doubt Me? Perhaps you have been let down by people you love who have made empty promises to you. You have been led astray by people who do not have your best interests in mind. You have been abandoned by a trusted friend in your hour of need. You have been left to fend for yourself because nobody else will take care of you properly. You hold onto control because you cannot bear further disappointment in those you depend on. I understand your doubts.

I am none of those things. I am the Lord your God. I will not let you down; I keep My promises. I will not lead you astray; I lead you down paths of righteousness for My name's sake. I will never leave you or forsake you in your hour of need. I am with you always. You do not have to be so strong; I will protect you and take care of you. Let go. I am in control. You can count on Me. I will not disappoint you. I am the one who created you to love you. You are My beloved child. You can depend on Me for all your needs. I will provide for you.

You are blessed when you believe what I tell you will be accomplished. I do not ask you to have faith in weak people who will most definitely disappoint you. I ask you to trust in Me, believe Me, and My will shall be done. I will do as I say, whether you believe Me or not; but when you believe Me, you will experience abundant blessings. My words are not empty. They do not come back to Me void. I speak, and the world obeys My commands. I spoke the world into existence.

Try putting your trust in Me completely. Give Me a chance. Bad things happen in the world, and I allow it for the good of those who love Me; but I will never leave you to fend for yourself. I wait for you to run to Me, and depend on Me for your life. It is during these difficult times that you understand how much you mean to Me. You appreciate My promises to be

---

[3] Sindy Nagel, "Believe Me" in *Manna for Today: Bread from Heaven for Each Day* (Bloomington, IN: WestBow Press 2012), 80.

true. You see that you are really not in control; but I am in command of all things.

The next time you hear My voice will you be ready to listen? Will you believe that what I say to you will be accomplished? Blessed be the one who believes wholeheartedly. Be expectant with the confidence of knowing I am who I say I am. I am Lord of lords and King of kings; yet you call Me Father. I am the Most High God—holy, holy, holy, yet you have direct access to Me. I am the Savior of the world, yet you call Me your friend. I AM. Believe what I say.

Self-Reflection:

1. Do you believe God will speak to you, or do you doubt it (believe the contrary)? Explain the basis for any doubt.

2. Do you desire to hear God's voice? What difference will it make in your life?

3. Do you believe Satan is responsible for introducing some of the thoughts you have? What evidence or support do you have for your answer?

4. Identify some lies that may be holding you in bondage, preventing you from hearing God's voice.

5. Find Scripture to refute every lie you listed above. Write out each verse and reference.

6. Now practice repeating the verses out loud. Satan does not know your thoughts, so it would be ineffective to rebuke him silently. Hold onto the truth in God's Word and draw on it again if you recognize these lies creeping back into your mind. Repeat them out loud every time you catch yourself listening to the lies of the devil.

7. Find and write out Scripture that proves Jesus Christ has given you power and authority over the devil. Now claim the truth in these verses as you repeat them aloud whenever necessary.

Removing the Barrier of Doubt

Ask God to expose the lies and help you identify any false beliefs that cause a barrier of doubt between you and God. Record them here.

Request that God bring memories to your mind of His presence in your life as it relates to your struggles with doubt. Pay close attention to what He is doing and saying to you in your thoughts. Write it down here.

Allow the Holy Spirit to lead you to Scripture verses that shine the light of God's truth into the deceptions you've believed. The concordance in your Bible comes in handy when you're searching for verses regarding a topic or word you hear from the Lord. Write the Bible verses and references here.

In the power given to you by Jesus Christ, through the shedding of His blood, take authority over the enemy and his attempts to distract and confuse you with his misconceptions. Speak out loud to rebuke the devil and proclaim the truth of God's Word, which you recorded above.

Pray:

Father in heaven, thank You for Your patience as I learn to trust in You. Thank You for chasing me in pursuit of intimate relationship. Thank You for Your gift of the Holy Spirit, Whom You sent to speak Your mind to me and make things known to me. Forgive me for my doubt in Your spoken Word, Your power, and/or Your promises. I long for two-way communication with You, and yet my doubt created a barrier between us. Lord, forgive me for believing any misrepresentations of the truth. Lord, I release my doubt and claim Your good truth in John 8:47: I am a child of God; therefore, I can hear what You say. Lord, I will make time to spend with You, listening to Your voice and knowing You more intimately. Father, press down Your truth in my spirit as I submit myself to Your Lordship. Hide me in the shadow of Your wings and protect me from the enemy, who tries to confuse me and deceive me. I claim the freedom You died to give me, and I place my confidence and trust in You alone. I pray this in the name of Your Son, Jesus. Amen.

Listen:

Lord, what do You want me to know about my doubt? (Write down all your thoughts and identify which thoughts may actually be God's voice.)

Chapter 2

Fear

The Enemy of Confidence

*For God did not give us a spirit of timidity,
but a spirit of power, of love and of self-discipline.
(2 Timothy 1:7)*

The only thing we have to fear is fear itself.
—Franklin D. Roosevelt

From God's Heart to Yours

My precious child, do not be afraid of the unknown. Do not fret about the mystery of My ways. Intimacy with Me is nothing to fear. I am not unapproachable. I love you and care for you more deeply than you will ever comprehend. I always look out for your best interests. I have plans to prosper you, not to harm you. I love you so much that I sent My only Son to die in your place. Your sin deserved death, but I have given you life through My Son.

Neither should you fear what I will say to you. I always know what you need to hear. Seek Me when you need advice. Consult Me when you need direction. Look to Me for the encouragement you desire. Come to Me when you need comfort. Listen to Me to receive wise counsel. Trust in Me, and discard your fears. My ways are higher than yours. Nothing comes to you that hasn't already been sifted through My hands. You are of great concern to Me. You are forever in My thoughts.

Dear, sweet friend, be anxious for nothing. I am in control of all things. Tell Me your greatest fears. Chances are good that they are rooted in lies you have heard from the evil one. I will show you the truth, and the truth will set you free from your apprehension. There is no fear in love, but My perfect love will cast out all your fears.

Spend time in My Word to know Me better. Do you know Jesus? If you know My Son, then you know Me. I and My Son are

One. Do you love Jesus? Then you love Me too. For I am in My Son and My Son is in Me.

Draw near to Me—do not be afraid. I am the Good Shepherd, and I call you by name. You are My sheep. I know My sheep, and My sheep know Me. Do not wander from the fold. I have great plans for you. I will not lead you astray. Trust in Me and cast all your cares upon Me. Come to Me for your rest. I will lead you beside still waters and calm your insecurities. Confidence in Me will soon replace your fear.

FEAR

Apprehension about the unknown can keep us from understanding the mystery of God. But fear is not from God. Second Timothy 1:7 says, "For God did not give us a spirit of timidity, but a spirit of power, of love and of self-discipline." I had a fear of God, but not the right kind of fear. Before I got to know God better, apprehension shrouded my desire to speak in conversation with Him. I feared that everything that came out of God's mouth would convict me. I dreaded His wrath, because I did not know the truth about His character.

God is loving, kind, compassionate, forgiving, faithful, trustworthy, and so much more. He loves us so much He wants to have an intimate relationship with each of us. I had to get to know God more intimately before the only fear I felt toward Him equaled awe and reverence. Psalm 147:11 says, "The Lord delights in those who fear Him, who put their hope in His unfailing love." God delights when we fear Him with a reverence that acknowledges we can put our trust in Him and depend on Him for everything.

Now that I know God better because of spending time in His Word and listening to His voice, I no longer fear Him with anxiety and apprehension. I can't wait to speak with Him because He amazes me. I now fear God out of reverence and respect because He has made His loving character known to me through His Word and His voice. I can depend on Him to meet all my needs. "The fear of the Lord is the beginning of wisdom" (Psalm 111:10).

Read Acts 9. It's the story of Saul, later renamed Paul. After the death and resurrection of Christ, Saul threatened to kill Jesus' disciples and take His followers as prisoners to Jerusalem. As he neared Damascus, however, he saw a light from heaven flash around him. "He fell to the ground and heard a voice say to him, 'Saul, Saul, why do you persecute Me?'" (Acts 9:4) It was the voice of Jesus. Saul could have fallen from the fear and dread of what was about to happen, or from the awe and reverence of being in the presence of the Lord. As he met the Lord face to face, Saul may have feared his own identity as one who persecuted the Jesus who stood before him.

Is it possible your identity causes you anxiety in communicating with Jesus? If you have accepted Jesus as your Savior, you are a child of God. No longer are you a slave to fear. Psalm 34:4 says, "I sought the Lord, and He answered me; He delivered me from all my fears." However, you may not feel connected to God. Maybe you've strayed from living a life that pleases God, and the shame you feel causes you to fear God's wrath. Perhaps you have stopped attending church, reading the Bible, or praying regularly. As a result, you experience apprehension about how Jesus would relate to you if He spoke to you.

Many times, we claim our identity from external sources in our lives. My identity branded me early in life when I heard my mom repeatedly refer to me as "an accident." Accidents are unwanted, unexpected events that we don't plan for and that sometimes cause pain: physical, emotional, or spiritual. I knew my mom had not planned me; therefore, I believed I was unwanted and unloved. My conception and birth had caused my mother undue emotional pain and then emotionally scarred me for much of my life. The external label "accident" spawned an internal insecurity about my identity that stuck with me for more than thirty years.

Another fear that blocked my communication with God was the fear of intimacy. I feared He wouldn't speak to me; therefore, I didn't want to experience the pain of rejection. I wasn't even sure He listened to me when I talked to Him. I hesitated to get emotionally close to God and become too dependent on Him because I feared He would let me down, as others had.

I knew I was a child of God, but I didn't *feel* like His child. *What if God also viewed me as an accident? What if He didn't love me either? What if my sins were too big for God to forgive? God wouldn't speak to me. I was nothing to Him. I was nobody special. Why would He talk to me?* Do you ever experience conversations like this within yourself? Are you insecure about your relationship with Jesus? Are you unsure about your identity in Christ? I was. My uncertainties caused me to approach the throne of God with fear and trembling, not in confidence with awe and wonder.

The first time I sat down to listen for God's voice, I needed reassurance from God that He wasn't angry with me. I wanted to know how He felt about me. I longed to know who He saw when He looked at me. I craved His attention, positive or negative. I prepared myself for whatever He would say to me. I wanted to know who I was to God and that He had a plan for my life. Battling depression for the second time, I desperately needed a reason to go on.

My depression counseling sessions had turned into spiritual mentoring meetings. My counselor described how he listened to Jesus's voice and encouraged me to try it. He instructed me to record my conversations with Jesus in a journal. During one session, we talked about how God has His own special name for each of His children. My counselor invited me to consider asking God, "What is your name for me?"

A name is more than a way to identify someone. It's a birthright; it represents our heritage, our legacy, our inheritance. It becomes our own challenge to make our names good and live up to our full potential as God's creation. This starts when we seek God for His name for us. We can't live into our God-given identity and purpose until we understand what that is.

God's chosen name for you may be different than the name your parents gave you. Let's explore a few people in the Bible who received their names, or identity, directly from the mouth of God.

1. God Himself named three people in Genesis 17. When Abram was ninety-nine years old, God established the covenant of circumcision with him and declared that he would be the father of many nations. In verse 5, God changed

Abram's name to Abraham, which means *father of many*. In verse 15, God changed Abram's wife's name from Sarai to Sarah, which means *princess*. God promised to bless her with a son, so that she would be the mother of nations, and kings would come from her. Abraham laughed at the idea that Sarah would bear a child at the age of ninety. After that, God instructed Abraham to name his son Isaac, which means *he laughs* (verse 19).

2. In Genesis 32:22-30, Jacob wrestled with God all night, until daybreak. Jacob would not let go of the Lord until He blessed him. God gave Jacob the new name Israel, which means *he struggles with God,* in verse 28.

3. In Luke 1:11-17, the angel Gabriel, who stood in the presence of God, instructed Zechariah to name his infant son John, which means *God is gracious*. John the Baptist, the cousin of Jesus, would prepare the way and make ready a people for the Lord by baptizing them in Jesus' name.

4. In Luke 1:26-33, God sent the angel Gabriel to the virgin Mary to inform her that the Holy Spirit would come upon her, His power overshadowing her, so that she would be with child. The holy one to be born would be the Son of the Most High God. Gabriel instructed her to give her baby the name Jesus, which means *the Lord saves*.

5. In Matthew 16:13-19, Jesus asked His disciples, "Who do you say I am?" Simon answered, "You are the Christ, the Son of the living God." Jesus declared Simon to be Peter, meaning *the rock*. Peter helped form the foundation of the church with Christ Jesus Himself as the chief cornerstone (see Ephesians 2:20).

6. As we've seen, in Acts 13:9, Saul, meaning *called of God*, was called Paul, meaning *humble*, after his conversion by

Jesus on the road to Damascus. Paul became the apostle chosen to carry Jesus' name before the Gentiles and their kings and before the people of Israel. Paul suffered greatly for the sake of Jesus' name, introducing many to the Lord's saving grace.

Considering the possibility that God had a special name for me, I was excited to learn it. It was the missing link to my identity, my sanity, and my confidence in Christ. One evening, I escaped the noise of my family and retired to my quiet bedroom. This marked the first time that I really tried to hear God speak. I wanted to capture whatever I heard from God that night, so I wrote all my thoughts in a notebook.

I asked God, "What do you think of me? Who am I to you? Do you have a name for me?" I listened intently but heard nothing. I kept asking the same questions but didn't know what to expect or how the answer would come to me. Would I hear an audible voice? Again I inquired of God, "Who do you see when you look at me? What is your name for me?"

In one very distinct moment, I heard in my thoughts, "Daughter of Zion." I wrote it down, but I quickly dismissed this name, not being able to relate to it at all. I asked God again, "What is your name for me?" Again, the voice in my head replied, "Daughter of Zion." Once more, I thought I'd heard it incorrectly. I couldn't identify with the name. I didn't understand its meaning. I had expected to hear a name like "beloved one," similar to the name one of my friend's had heard.

A third time, I requested God's name for me. Yet again, God confirmed it: "DAUGHTER OF ZION." I heard it in my thoughts, and this time the words took center stage in my head, displayed in all capital letters. Three times God clearly spoke the same name to me in my thoughts. I knew it must be the name He had given me—but I didn't recognize the meaning behind it.

One way to confirm and comprehend what God says to us is to go to Scripture. Using the concordance in my Bible, I began a two-hour search for all the verses and meanings I could find about the words "Daughter of Zion" and "Zion." Seeing these words appear in more than twenty-five verses surprised me. As I read each verse and the surrounding passages, a feeling of peace and joy came over me. Emotion overwhelmed me. When I discovered the meaning of God's name for me, it resonated with me. This name would most likely not mean the same thing to any other person, but it embodied everything I longed to be to God and everything I desired to hear from God at that moment.

Here are some examples of the "Zion" verses and surrounding passages. The identity I gleaned from each verse or passage appears italicized below it.

Psalm 2:6, "I have installed My King on Zion, My holy hill."

God is the King in Zion and I am His daughter—that makes me a princess.

Zechariah 2:10, "Shout and be glad, O Daughter of Zion. For I am coming, and I will live among you," declares the Lord.

God, my King, comes for me and lives in me. I am glad!

Zephaniah 3:14-17, "Sing, O Daughter of Zion; shout aloud, O Israel! Be glad and rejoice with all your heart, O Daughter of Jerusalem! The Lord has taken away your punishment, He has turned back your enemy. The Lord, the King of Israel, is with you; never again will you fear any harm. On that day they will say to Jerusalem, 'Do not fear, O Zion; do not let your hands hang limp. The Lord your God is with you, He is mighty to save. He will take great delight in you, He will quiet you with His love, He will rejoice over you with singing.'"

I will be glad and rejoice, for my God is with me, delights in me, loves me, and rejoices over me. He takes away my depression and rebukes my enemy. He is with me; I will not fear.

Psalm 132:13-15, "For the Lord has chosen Zion, He has desired it for His dwelling: 'This is My resting place for ever and ever; here I will sit enthroned, for I have desired it—I will bless her with abundant provisions; her poor will I satisfy with food.'"

God chose me and lives in me forever. He desires me and blesses me abundantly.

Isaiah 43:1, "Fear not, for I have redeemed you; I have called you by name; you are Mine."

God redeemed me and called me by name; I am His.

Psalm 69:35, "For God will save Zion."

He will save me.

Isaiah 51:3, "The Lord will surely comfort Zion and will look with compassion on all her ruins; He will make her deserts like Eden, her wastelands like the garden of the Lord. Joy and gladness will be found in her, thanksgiving and the sound of singing."

He Himself will comfort me and have compassion on me. He will turn my loneliness into joy, gladness, and thanksgiving.

Isaiah 28:16, "So this is what the Sovereign Lord says, 'See, I lay a stone in Zion, a tested stone, a precious cornerstone for a sure foundation; the one who trusts will never be dismayed.'"

Jesus is my cornerstone, my sure foundation. When I trust in Him, I will not be depressed.

Isaiah 62:11-12, The Lord has made proclamation to the ends of the earth: "Say to the Daughter of Zion, 'See, your Savior comes! See, His reward is with Him, and His recompense accompanies Him.' They will be called The Holy People, The Redeemed of the Lord; and you will be called Sought After, The City No Longer Deserted.'"

Jesus, my Savior, comes for me with His reward. I am redeemed and sought after, no longer left alone.

Isaiah 62:1-4, "For Zion's sake I will not keep silent, for Jerusalem's sake I will not remain quiet, till her righteousness shines out like the dawn, her salvation like a blazing torch. The nations will see your righteousness, and all kings your glory; you will be called by a new name that the mouth of the Lord will bestow. You will be a crown of splendor in the Lord's hand, a royal diadem in the hand of your God. No longer will they call you Deserted, or name your land

Desolate. But you will be called Hephzibah, and your land Beulah; for the Lord will take delight in you, and your land will be married."

The Lord calls me by a new name. No longer am I alone or lonely. He delights in me.

Isaiah 35:10, "And the ransomed of the Lord will return. They will enter Zion with singing; everlasting joy will crown their heads. Gladness and joy will overtake them, and sorrow and sighing will flee away."

Everlasting joy will crown my head; sorrow and sadness will flee.

Psalm 102:13, 16, 21, "You will arise and have compassion on Zion, for it is time to show favor to her…For the Lord will rebuild Zion and appear in His glory…So the name of the Lord will be declared in Zion."

The Lord will have compassion on me, show His favor to me, and rebuild me. He will be glorified because I will declare His name and what He has done for me.

That evening, God met me at the bottom of the pit of depression I occupied. He showered me with His loving kindness. He lifted me up out of the darkness and washed off the mud. I connected with Him in a way I never had before. He isn't only an authority figure who lives in heaven and disciplines me when I need it. He isn't just a figurehead for me to worship.

I had a new understanding that **God is alive**. He's a loving Father who cares about me and wants to have a relationship with me. I felt special, wanted, and loved by God. I felt important to God, a priority to Him. When I discovered how God felt about me, nothing else mattered. My fear dissipated and my confidence in the Lord replaced it. When I felt loved and wanted by the God of the universe, I had a new reason to live and a new excitement about what the future would hold for me.

Not only did the name give me my identity in God's family, but it exploded with explanation and meaning of who I am to God and Who He is to me. It summed up exactly what I needed to know. No longer did I fear spending time with God.

Earlier, in a state of depression, I had a low opinion of myself. The enemy had stripped me of everything good that God had created in me and left me cracked and broken. God knew my desperate need. As I sought Him more, He began rebuilding me from the ground up. The Most High Himself established me. I had been holding onto my faith by a thread, and hearing God's voice confirmed my belief in a God who is real—not just real, but *alive.*

The name God gave me clarified not only my identity as His child, but also His identity and His character. God, my Rescuer, freed me from the captivity of Satan's lies by replacing them with His perfect truth. God, my Healer and Restorer, sealed the cracks in my vessel and rebuilt my character. God, my Comforter, consoled me Himself. God, my Immanuel, made my heart His dwelling place so He is always with me. God, my Restorer, removed my sackcloth and clothed me with joy. God, my Deliverer, turned back my enemies and showed His favor to me. God, my Friend, pursued me and spent time with me.

Shortly after I received God's name for me and began spending more time alone with Him, my church went through a *40 Days of Purpose* study from the book *The Purpose Driven Life* by Rick Warren. From this study, God revealed and confirmed many things to me as He healed me and strengthened me.

God brought to light the reason He created me and His purpose for my life here on earth. He wants me to help set His captives free, like He set me free, by awakening hearts to Him. He wants me to help lead His people to the promised land, which is the abundant life in Christ, through a personal, intimate relationship with Him. He wants me to be a light to the Gentiles, people who do not know God yet. Really, these assignments represent activities He calls all of His children to carry out. It's what Jesus did when He walked the earth. God's Word promises, in John 14:12, we will do even greater things than Jesus did. Can you believe it?

This entire process, God's refining work in me, started with His wisdom in allowing me to experience difficult times in life, including depression. Once He had my attention and I responded with complete dependence on Him, He had access to my pliable heart and mind. He knocked at the door of my heart once more, and this time, my heart jumped into action. I opened the door and let Him in. He sat with me, and I sat with Him. I responded to Him with an increased desire to know Him more. I began to seek God with all my heart, soul, mind, and strength. I found Him, and I learned to quiet myself enough to hear His voice.

If you have not yet heard the voice of God, I encourage you to listen. If you do not yet know God's name for you, I pray you will ask Him. If you find yourself imprisoned by Satan's lies about your identity, I invite you to seek God's truth and let God Himself set you straight.

God is a gentleman. He pursues us, but He doesn't crash in on us and take us over. In Revelation 3:20, Jesus says, "Here I am! I stand at the door and knock. If anyone hears My voice and opens the door, I will come in and eat with him, and he with Me." Jesus continually pursues us. He is pursuing you now. He stands at the door to your heart and knocks, saying, "Here I am!" He patiently waits for you to listen, hear His voice, open the door, and let Him in to enjoy intimate relationship with the living God.

Open the door to Jesus. He will come in, sit with you, and eat with you. Are you hungry to hear God's voice? Are you desperate enough to listen? He waits for your response. Will you open your door, and your ears, to what God has to say to you? He calls you by name. No need to fear God because of who you are or who you are not. You are His child, loved and redeemed by Him. Identify yourself with the name God so carefully chose for you before the world began. Your name is engraved on His palms (see Isaiah 49:16).

God-Given Name Exercise

God desires to spend time with you and show you how much He loves you. He wants you to know who you are to Him—who He created you to be. God has a special name for you that may be different than the name your parents gave you. Take time this week to ask God to answer these questions for you. Listen to His voice, and write down the thoughts He gives you. Start by writing down the very first thing that comes to mind after you ask Him these questions. Write it down no matter how unusual it may seem. God's name for you is not always a person's name; it could be an attribute, characteristic, or special gift.

In your quiet time with the Lord, ask Him these questions and record the thoughts that immediately come to your mind:

1. God, what is Your name for me?

2. God, who am I to You—who do You see when You look at me?

3. God, what do You think of me?

4. God, please show me Bible verses that help me understand what this name means and what I mean to You. Lord, also show me who You are to me. (Use your Bible concordance to find verses that relate to your name and what you hear God say.)

5. We all have multiple names that identify who we are in Christ: Forgiven, Beloved, Blessed One, etc. List some other names that describe a believer's identity in Christ and

determine the power that comes with each name you've listed.

6. What responsibilities do God-given names or identities carry? Give some examples.

7. How might the purpose God creates us for align with the name He gives us? Provide examples from people God named in the Scripture passages we discussed in this chapter.

If you do not hear God's voice or His name for you this time, don't give up. Keep pursuing Him until you recognize His voice and hear His name for you. It may be that God speaks to you and you don't hear Him. Or He may be waiting for a very special time in the future to reveal your identity in Jesus Christ. Read a few more chapters, and then try asking God these questions again. Be open to whatever you hear Him say. Try not to have any preconceived ideas about what your name will be. Do not compare your God-given name to His name for someone else. He will give you exactly the name that identifies you for His purposes.

We have multiple names for the ones we love, such as honey, dear, sweetheart, precious, and babe. God also has multiple names for the ones He loves. If He has already given you a name, ask Him for an additional name and the identity, purpose, or responsibility that comes with it. Write down what you hear.

There is power in the name of Jesus, and likewise, the name Jesus bestows on you empowers your identity in Him. When you hear His name for you, dive into learning what the name means for your identity and your God-given purpose.

As you practice listening to God's voice and hearing His name for you, your enemy may attempt to distract you with his personal signature of deceit. Consider the three lies below as just a sampling of the tools Satan carries in his tool belt. Think about your personal weaknesses. Your enemy will certainly strike you where you are most vulnerable. Find the holes in your armor that may have left you exposed and defenseless in the past. Be on the alert and ready to battle Satan's lies with the truth from God's Word. Pre-plan your method of defense, and arm yourself with Scripture verses that you will use to voice the truth, dispelling the devil's distractions of deceit.

LIE #1: The only thing God has to say to you is to convict you of your sin.

Satan, not God, loves to convict you *and condemn you* of your sin. He relishes the thought of a child of God wallowing in his or her own guilt and shame. Most assuredly, Satan will add fuel to your remorse fire and stir the coals of your prolonged disgrace well past your period of repentance. His subtle reminders of your misdeeds can erect bars on the windows of your soul, holding you captive in the prison of not accepting God's forgiveness for your sin and minimizing the death of Jesus as your recompense.

Your enemy, the devil, would love for you to invest in the idea that you should fear God's conviction, so much so that you altogether avoid attempting to listen to God's voice. One role of the Holy Spirit is to "convict the world of guilt in regard to sin and righteousness and judgment; in regard to sin, because men do not believe in Me," as Jesus says in John 16:8-9. While it's true that the Holy Spirit points out our offenses that is not the only thing God sent Him here to accomplish. God has a lot more to say to you. His interest in helping you live a sanctified life far outweighs His desire to pass daily judgment regarding your offenses. As a loving parent gently corrects a disobedient child, the Holy Spirit makes us aware of our waywardness to keep us on a path of righteousness and redemption.

TRUTH #1: God loves to encourage you, impart His wisdom, guide you, love on you, and give you His peace.

As quoted earlier in John 16:13-15, Jesus also explained that the Spirit of truth will guide us into truth, speak what He hears from God, and inform us of what is to come. He'll bring glory to Jesus by making the things of the Father known to us. Further, in John 14:26, Jesus says, "But the Counselor, the Holy Spirit, Whom the Father will send in My name, will teach you all things and will remind you of everything I have said to you."

The Holy Spirit, Who is from God, fills many positions and titles, for example Counselor, Comforter, Advocate, Teacher, Reminder, Speaker, Leader, Guide, Spirit of Truth, Life, Peace, Encourager, Motivator, Healer, Helper, Intercessor, Giver of Spiritual Gifts, and Producer of the Fruit of the Spirit. As the Spirit carries out all these roles, He speaks to us according to what He hears from God and Jesus. Therefore, you will most definitely hear more than conviction from the mouth of God.

The Truth in God's Word:

May our Lord Jesus Christ Himself and God our Father, Who loved us and by His grace gave us eternal encouragement and good hope, encourage your hearts and strengthen you in every good deed and word. (2 Thessalonians 2:16-17)

Then you will understand the fear of the Lord and find the knowledge of God. For the Lord gives wisdom, and from His mouth come knowledge and understanding. (Proverbs 2:5-6)

No, we speak of God's secret wisdom, a wisdom that has been hidden and that God destined for our glory before time began. None of the rulers of this age understood it, for if they had, they would not have crucified the Lord of glory. However, as it is written:

> "No eye has seen, no ear has heard, and no mind has conceived what God has prepared for those who love Him"—

But *God has revealed to us by His Spirit. The Spirit searches all things, even the deep things of God. For who among men knows the thoughts of a man except the man's spirit within him? In the same way no one knows the thoughts of God except the Spirit of God. We have not received the spirit of the world but the Spirit Who is from God, that we may understand what God has freely given us.* This is what we speak, not in words taught us by human wisdom but in words taught by the Spirit, expressing spiritual truths in spiritual words. The man without the Spirit does not accept the things that come from the Spirit of God, for they are foolishness to him, and he cannot understand them, because they are spiritually discerned. The spiritual man makes judgments about all things, but he himself is not subject to any man's judgment:

> "For who has known the mind of the Lord that he may instruct Him?"

But *we have the mind of Christ.* (1 Corinthians 2:7-16; emphasis mine)

Trust in the Lord with all your heart and lean not on your own understanding; in all your ways acknowledge Him, and He will make your paths straight. Do not be wise in your own eyes; fear the Lord and shun evil. This will bring health to your body and nourishment to your bones. (Proverbs 3:5-8)

"All this I have spoken while still with you. But the Counselor, the Holy Spirit, Whom the Father will send in My name, will teach you all things and will remind you of everything I have said to you. Peace I leave with you; My peace I give you. I do not give to you as the world gives. *Do not let your hearts be troubled and do not be afraid.*" (John 14:25-27; emphasis mine)

LIE

#2: If you listen to God, He'll ask you to do something you don't want to do—like become an overseas missionary.

I'll be the first to admit I was a bit apprehensive about listening to God because I feared He might inform me I had to work overseas as a missionary on a remote continent with people for whom I had no affinity. While that may be true on rare occasions, most often God will not send you to a foreign nation without preparing your mind and heart for His specific purposes.

I will also confess that God's purposes for me and the tasks He assigns to me align with things I never thought possible—and rightfully so. I couldn't accomplish them if not for the power of God's Spirit within me. But when God matures us through difficult times in our lives, He fulfills His promise in Romans 8:28: "And we know that in all things God works for the good of those who love Him, who have been called according to His purpose." You can be sure if God calls you, He will equip you for the task, whatever it may be.

For example, I possessed such a great fear of public speaking that I never dreamed God would require that of me. Since Jesus turned my test into a testimony, though, I can't keep quiet about His goodness. By the power of the Holy Spirit, I now stand with confidence in front of crowds sharing His work in my life and inspiring others to enjoy a greater intimacy with Him. It's also the assignments I fear the most that bring the greatest joy when I have been obedient to God and completed His will—probably because I know the Spirit is at work in and through me, and that is an awesome experience.

TRUTH #2: God created us in Christ Jesus to do good works, which He prepared in advance for us to do.

Chapter one listed some examples of ordinary people from the Old Testament whom God spoke to directly. I do realize that most of these average Joes became significant characters in Bible history, but none of them started out that way. It was because they listened to and obeyed God that He could use them for His divine purposes even though they were still human and sinful.

Before He formed the earth, God had you in mind (see Ephesians 1:4). He had a purpose for creating you and He created you for a purpose (see Ephesians 1:11). In the words of Rick Warren, "If you want to know why you were placed on this planet, you must begin with God. You were born *by* His purpose and *for* His purpose."[4] Not everyone to whom God speaks was created to do missionary work in a foreign land. You won't know the purpose God created you for until you hear Him tell you or watch Him show you.

It may not be just one big all-consuming single life purpose. It could be a series of small activities or actions woven together to fulfill an as-yet-unknown purpose. In any case, you can be sure all the days ordained for you were in God's plan before one of them came to be (see Psalm 139:16). Be careful not to compare your purpose with that of others. No purpose is greater or lesser than another. Your purpose is exactly right for you. God prepares you and equips you to carry out His plans. Whatever the purpose is, big or small, simple or complex, He wants to help you live into the fullness of the life that He designed for you—the full life that Jesus Christ came to give you.

Proverbs 19:21 says, "Many are the plans in a man's heart, but it is the Lord's purpose that prevails." When we discover God's purpose for our lives, we should re-purpose our lives for God. Find your wisdom and your strength from the source of all power, and listen to the voice of God within you. He has great plans for you, "plans to prosper you and not to harm you, plans to give you hope and a future" (Jeremiah 29:11).

"Come near to God and He will come near to you" (James 4:8). He will fill your heart with exactly what you need, equipping

---

[4] Rick Warren, *The Purpose Driven Life*, (Grand Rapids, MI: Zondervan, 2002), 17.

you with confidence and conviction to do His good and perfect will. You have what it takes. You are enough. Delight yourself in the Lord, Who invites you into an exciting personal adventure in Him for now and all eternity. Experience life in the fullest, the way God intended. Do not allow Satan to diminish the value of your God-given purpose by causing you to be afraid of God and what He might say to you when you listen to Him.

The Truth in God's Word:

And we know that in all things God works for the good of those who love Him, who have been called according to His purpose. For those God foreknew He also predestined to be conformed to the likeness of His Son, that He might be the firstborn among many brothers. And those He predestined, He also called; those He called, He also justified; those He justified, He also glorified. (Romans 8:28-30)

For it is God who works in you to will and to act according to His good purpose. (Philippians 2:13)

In Him we were also chosen, having been predestined according to the plan of Him Who works out everything in conformity with the purpose of His will, in order that we, who were the first to hope in Christ, might be for the praise of His glory. And you also were included in Christ when you heard the word of truth, the gospel of your salvation. Having believed, you were marked in Him with a seal, the promised Holy Spirit, Who is a deposit guaranteeing our inheritance until the redemption of those who are God's possession—to the praise of His glory. (Ephesians 1:11-14)

For we are God's workmanship, created in Christ Jesus to do good works, which God prepared in advance for us to do. (Ephesians 2:10)

It was He Who gave some to be apostles, some to be prophets, some to be evangelists, and some to be pastors and teachers, to prepare God's people for works of service, so that the body of Christ may be built up until we all reach unity in the faith and in the knowledge of the Son of God and become mature, attaining to the whole measure of the fullness of Christ. (Ephesians 4:11-13)

LIE #3: You are a sinner, and God is full of wrath and fury toward those who have sinned.

If your reading of God's Word is limited to the Old Testament, or even if you stopped reading after the first book, Genesis, I could see why you might fear God's wrath and fury toward the sinner. In Genesis 6, people had become so wicked and evil that God was sorry He had made them. He spared only Noah's family and two of every animal on the ark when He sent a flood to wipe out all of humankind. Then, in Genesis 19, the Lord rained down burning sulfur on Sodom and Gomorrah, destroying everyone in both cities because their sin was so grievous. Next, He turned Lot's wife into a pillar of salt because she disobeyed Him. Certainly, one might be justified in fearing a God who could destroy His own creation in these ways.

Truly, sin makes God angry and causes Him to hide His face from the sinner. Our wickedness distances us from Him. However, we cannot forget or minimize God's wonderful plan of salvation. When you thoroughly ponder the amazing, sacrificial act planned by God and carried out by His Son, Jesus, you begin to understand the depth of God's great love for all of His creation, and that includes Y-O-U. The God of the universe took on the form of a man, by sending His one and only Son to earth. He was born of a virgin and lived a sin-free life so that He could be the perfect sacrifice to pay our debt in full, once and for all. Allowing His Son to hang on a cross as a sacrificial Lamb of atonement was an enormously selfless act on God's part. When we really think about this perfect plan for our salvation, we cannot help realizing that God possesses more of a boundless love than a ferocious fury for His children in spite of all our sin. He is not angry and wrathful at all times. Still, we can expect to suffer the natural, earthly consequences of our poor decisions, bad choices, and disobedience.

In addition, let's not confuse God's wrath with His purpose when it comes to our trials and suffering. We know that God allows His children to experience difficult times, disease, natural disasters, and unpleasant circumstances in order to mature us in our faith. His thoughts are higher than our thoughts, and His ways are higher than our ways (see Isaiah 55:9). Our omniscient Father sees the grand picture: past, present, and future. He created a divine plan for the whole world and everyone in it. He knows what's best for us, and

He's willing to use all circumstances for the good of those who love Him, who have been called according to His purpose (see Romans 8:28).

The best response we can offer God during our trials is to thank Him and ask Him to use them to increase our faith and trust in Him. Most likely, the purpose and result of your test are interwoven with the purpose and test of many other people at the same time. God intricately weaves together the threads of our lives so that multiple aspects of His plan are accomplished in what seems like a single purpose or event but involves many people at once, far exceeding what we will ever realize or comprehend.

TRUTH

#3: While it's true God does not like sin, He rejoices over the sinner who repents. In fact, God pursues the lost and celebrates when the lost are found.

Read these excerpts from the parables that Jesus relayed to the Pharisees in Luke 15.

The Parable of the Lost Sheep

> "Suppose one of you has a hundred sheep and loses one of them. Does he not leave the ninety-nine in the open country and go after the lost sheep until he finds it? And when he finds it, he joyfully puts it on his shoulders and goes home. Then he calls his friends and neighbors together and says, 'Rejoice with me; I have found my lost sheep.' I tell you that

in the same way there is more rejoicing in heaven over one sinner who repents than over ninety-nine righteous persons who do not need to repent." (Luke 15:4-7)

The Parable of the Lost Coin

"Or suppose a woman has ten silver coins and loses one. Does she not light a lamp, sweep the house and search carefully until she finds it? And when she finds it, she calls her friends and neighbors together and says, 'Rejoice with me; I have found my lost coin.' In the same way, I tell you, there is rejoicing in the presence of the angels of God over one sinner who repents." (Luke 15:8-10)

The Parable of the Lost Son

Jesus continued: "There was a man who had two sons. The younger one said to his father, 'Father, give me my share of the estate.' So he divided his property between them.

"Not long after that, the younger son got together all he had, set off for a distant country and there squandered his wealth in wild living. After he had spent everything, there was a severe famine in that whole country, and he began to be in need. So he went and hired himself out to a citizen of that country, who sent him to his fields to feed pigs. He longed to fill his stomach with the pods that the pigs were eating, but no one gave him anything.

"When he came to his senses, he said, 'How many of my father's hired men have food to spare, and here I am starving to death! I will set out and go back to my father and say to him: Father, I have sinned against heaven and against you. I am no longer worthy to be called your son; make me like one of your hired men.' So he got up and went to his father.

"But while he was still a long way off, his father saw him and was filled with compassion for him; he ran to his son, threw his arms around him and kissed him.

"The son said to him, 'Father, I have sinned against heaven and against you. I am no longer worthy to be called your son.'

"But the father said to his servants, 'Quick! Bring the best robe and put it on him. Put a ring on his finger and sandals on his feet. Bring the fattened calf and kill it. Let's have a feast and celebrate. For this son of mine was dead and is alive again; he was lost and is found.' So they began to celebrate." (Luke 15:11-24)

In all three parables above, the lost refers to the sinner, one who has strayed, been disobedient, or followed a path of evil rather than righteousness. And in all three cases, the one who represents God the Father rejoices when the lost sinner is found, repents, and returns to Him. Yes, God does not like sin, but He still loves the lost. His heart is for His children, and He is overjoyed when any one of them turns from wickedness and asks for forgiveness. His arms open wide to welcome back into His fold the one who has gone astray and then returns to Him. Let the celebration begin!

The Truth in God's Word:

"I tell you that in the same way there is more rejoicing in heaven over one sinner who repents than over ninety-nine righteous persons who do not need to repent." (Luke 15:7)

"In the same way, I tell you, there is rejoicing in the presence of the angels of God over one sinner who repents." (Luke 15:10)

"The son said to him, 'Father, I have sinned against heaven and against you. I am no longer worthy to be called your son.' But the father said to his servants, 'Quick! Bring the best robe and put it on him. Put a ring on his finger and sandals on his feet. Bring the fattened calf and kill it. Let's have a feast and celebrate. For this son of mine was dead and is alive again; he was lost and is found.' So they began to celebrate." (Luke 15:21-24)

Following are excerpts from my devotional book, ***Manna for Today: Bread from Heaven for Each Day***. These are examples of the words God spoke to me as I met with Him alone and listened to His voice. The three inspirations cited here fit well with the topic of fear.

There is no fear in love. But perfect love drives out fear, because fear has to do with punishment. The man who fears is not made perfect in love. (1 John 4:18) "Peace I leave with you; my peace I give you. I do not give to you as the world gives. Do not let your hearts be troubled and do not be afraid" (John 14:27).

Be Not Afraid[5]

My child, do not be afraid of what will be. Your life is too short to spend a moment entertaining anxious thoughts about what tomorrow will bring. Cast all your cares and burdens upon me. Let me worry about tomorrow. I will bear your burdens. I will carry you because I love you. I have loved you with an everlasting love. My love is perfect. Were you to understand the depth of My love for you, worry would no longer remain in your heart. Consider this: I laid down My life for you. I stood in the gap for a fallen world. There is no greater love than this. My perfect love drives out your fear. You must know Me better, to understand Me better. Spend time with Me to know Me. I am love. I am patient and kind. I am not easily angered. I do not keep a record of your wrongs. I will protect you. I will not fail you. I am here for you. Allow Me to love you out of your fear.

Will you accept the peace I have to give you? I do not give to you as the world gives. My love is not conditional. I love you no matter what. There is nothing you can do to make Me love you more. There is nothing you can do to make Me love you less. My love for you is constant and unconditional. My love is the most excellent gift I have to give you. Without My love, you are nothing. When you know Me and understand Me, you will accept My love for its worth. My love is sufficient for you. I am all you need. Cast Me not away. Draw near to Me, and I will draw near to you. Let Me love you, and do not be afraid.

Accept the peace I give you. It's not like anything you have ever experienced. It will surpass everything you currently understand about peace. You will have no worries believing that I am in control and trusting Me for everything. Nothing will clutter your mind and heart.

✝

---

[5] Sindy Nagel, "Be Not Afraid" in *Manna for Today: Bread from Heaven for Each Day* (Bloomington, IN: WestBow Press 2012), 78.

"The fear of the Lord is the beginning of wisdom, and knowledge of the Holy One is understanding" (Proverbs 9:10).

Know Me[6]

Do not fear Me as you would fear being alone in a cage with a hungry lion, but fear Me out of reverence for Me. You fear the lion because you know he is dangerously powerful. He is strong, confident, and his jaws are crushing. His fierce brawn, along with the mane he boasts around his head, entitles him to be called, "king of the jungle."

I am the lion of Judah—the King of kings. I am strong, confident, and powerful, too. What distinguishes Me from the lion you fear is that I love you, and desire the best for you. I would not hurt you or devour you. You are My beloved child—My own creation.

I desire your reverence. Respect My strength and My power. I can move mountains and cause them to crumble into the sea, but I care for you deeply, and would not use My power maliciously to destroy you. Your admiration of Me is the establishment of your wisdom. When you know Me, you will understand Me. When you know Me and understand Me, My wisdom is available to you. Ask Me for My wisdom, and I will give it to you freely. Respect Me, and My knowledge will be granted to you.

To know Me and understand Me, spend time with Me each day. The more time you spend with Me, the better you know Me. The better you know Me, the better you will understand Me. I am with you always. I know you better than you know yourself, but I still desire to spend as much time as possible with you each day, because I love you. You bring Me great joy when you seek Me and talk to Me. When you delight yourself in Me, I will give you the desires of your heart. I love to hear your voice—do you love to hear Mine? I love to just "be" with you. Give your time and your heart to Me, and you will be wise. My wisdom is available to all who know Me.

✝

---

[6] Sindy Nagel, "Know Me" in *Manna for Today: Bread from Heaven for Each Day* (Bloomington, IN: WestBow Press 2012), 99.

"The Lord your God is with you, He is mighty to save. He will take great delight in you, He will quiet you with His love, He will rejoice over you with singing" (Zephaniah 3:17).

I Take Great Delight in You[7]

O daughter of the King, you will rejoice and be glad. I have removed your punishment. You shall not be afraid of anything. I have turned back your enemy. I am with you, and will never leave you. I am powerful, and I will save you. You are My child, and I delight in you greatly. You are My daughter, My precious one. I will rescue you and bring you home. I will set you free from captivity.

O child of Mine, you are at home with Me. I enjoy the time I spend with you. You bring Me great pleasure and satisfaction. Do not let your heart be troubled. I will quiet you with My love. Do not set yourself to worry. I will remove all your cares. I will speak over you with My tender, soothing words. Listen to My gentle whispers. My voice will calm your uncertainties. I am here to protect you and save you. You have nothing to fear, for I am with you. I will not leave you alone.

O daughter of Mine, you are very special to Me. I will return the smile to your face. I rejoice over you with singing. My words fall quickly to your ears as you listen with great anticipation. I celebrate your presence. Your existence completes My joy. Rejoice and be glad with Me. Your heart will soar to new heights. I will set you on wings of eagles. Put your hope and trust in Me. I will renew your strength. I have led you out of your captivity and set you free. I will guide you, and arm you with My strength. I will surround you with My love, and protect you from your enemy.

O precious child of Mine, do you know how greatly I delight in you? Let Me quiet you with My love. Listen to Me as I rejoice over you in song. Let the sound of My voice be your comfort. Let My whispers calm your fears and reassure you of My great love for you.

✝

---

[7] Sindy Nagel, "I Take Great Delight in You" in *Manna for Today: Bread from Heaven for Each Day* (Bloomington, IN: WestBow Press 2012), 105.

Self-Reflection:

1. List some prominent fears you have with regard to hearing God speak to you:

2. Spend some time alone with God asking Him to speak to one of your fears. Record the thoughts the Holy Spirit gives you regarding this uncertainty. Also record the words from any Scripture that comes to mind.

3. Identify some of your thoughts about communicating with God that may actually be distractions or lies of the enemy.

4. Search your Bible concordance for verses that speak God's truth to the fears and lies you cited above. Write the verses and references here. Memorize these verses or keep them handy to be used as needed. Remember, it will be most effective to say the verses out loud as you expose the lies of the enemy.

5. Write down ten of your favorite characteristics, names, or attributes of God, Jesus, and the Holy Spirit. Consult Scripture if you need help thinking of some. For example: patient, kind, faithful, Immanuel, etc.

6. Choose one of the attributes listed above and write out a message to God thanking Him for filling that role in your life. Include a specific example of a time when God exercised that characteristic with you.

7. Identify one of God's purposes for your life. If you're unsure, ask God right now to speak about His plans for you. Listen to His voice within, and record what you hear. Confirm what you have heard by searching for related Bible verses through your concordance. List the verses that stand out to you, look them up, and meditate on them.

Removing the Barrier of Fear

Ask God to expose the lies and help you identify any false beliefs that cause a barrier of fear between you and God. Record them here.

Request that God bring memories to your mind of His presence in your life as it relates to your struggles with fear. Pay close attention to what He is doing and saying to you in your thoughts. Write it down here.

Allow the Holy Spirit to lead you to Scripture verses that shine the light of God's truth into the deceptions you've believed. The concordance in your Bible comes in handy when you're searching for verses regarding a topic or word you hear from the Lord. Write the Bible verses and references here.

In the power given to you by Jesus Christ, through the shedding of His blood, take authority over the enemy and his attempts to distract and confuse you with his misconceptions. Speak out loud to rebuke the devil and proclaim the truth of God's Word, which you recorded above.

Pray:

Precious Lord, I approach Your throne in awe and reverence. You are awesome in power, and Mighty is Your name. Thank You for loving me through my concerns. Please forgive my belief in that which causes my fear. Your perfect love drives out my fear. Thank You for pursuing me when I was lost. I desire to hear Your voice and words of love, kindness, encouragement, wisdom, and guidance. I know You created me for a purpose, and I pray You will equip me to carry out the works You prepared in advance for me to do. Your thoughts and Your ways are higher than mine, and You always know what's best for me. I submit my spirit to Your leading and declare You as my Lord. I lay down my fears at the foot of the cross, and I will fight to not pick them up again. You are my Fortress and my Shield. You protect me from the evil one. Of whom shall I be afraid when You are on my side? I will remain alert and try not to entertain the lies of the enemy. I will rebuke him with the truth found in You and Your Word. I pray this with the all power and authority given to me in the name of Jesus. Amen.

Listen:

Lord, what do You want me to know about my fear? (Write down all your thoughts and identify which thoughts may actually be God's voice.)

Chapter 3

Pride

The Enemy of Humility

A man's pride brings him low, but a man of lowly spirit gains honor. (Proverbs 29:23)

Pride makes us artificial and humility makes us real.
—Thomas Merton

From God's Heart to Yours

Cherished one, do not run ahead on your own, making plans for yourself. The best-laid plans can be disastrous when you do not walk in My will. I am in control of all things. I hung the moon and the stars in the sky and named each one. The heavens are my showplace. I created the earth and set it into orbit around the sun. All creation came to life by the commands of My lips. I instruct the ocean tides to advance and recede. I formed you in your mother's womb, and I know the number of your days. Why is it, then, that you believe you are in control of your own life? Your prideful ways are an abomination to Me.

I detest a haughty spirit. Arrogance erects a wall that blocks a good relationship with Me. Humble yourself, and I will exalt you. Take the position of the lowly one, and I will lift you up. Let go of all pride and submit yourself to Me.

Do not look down upon your brother or your sister, your neighbor or your friend. Judgment is Mine alone. Do not consider yourself better than another for any reason. I have created you all equally good. Trade in your selfish ways and become more selfless in nature. Humility will take you much farther than vain conceit in this life.

Serve Me with a contrite heart, and find Me in your presence. But rear the ugliness of pride, and I will distance Myself from you. Do not be so anxious to be self-sufficient, when I promise to supply all your needs. Independence receives worldly accolades, but I reward your dependence on Me.

Jesus lived a humble existence. You would do well to imitate His life in word and in deed. If you want to be exalted, become the servant. If you want to be lifted up, regard others as better than yourself. Respect everyone and extend the hand of mercy rather than judgment.

You were created in My image. I am a servant King. Reflect My glory by imitating Christ. I do not ask you to do something I have not done Myself. I reward the submissive spirit.

PRIDE

Independence, control, and comparison. Those words don't sound prideful when spoken alone. However, when we rely on ourselves for everything and don't depend on God for anything, He could view this independent spirit as arrogance or overconfidence. Likewise, it often feels good to be in complete control of ourselves, our lives, an event, a situation, another person, or his actions. The haughty monster of pride rears its ugly head in the condescending creature of control. And when we compare ourselves to others and always come out on top, a conceited nature triumphs over humility in our souls. Be careful—this sounds a bit like sitting in the judgment seat, and that's not a position you want to claim for yourself. Judgment is reserved for Almighty God alone.

Pride is mentioned in Proverbs 6:16-19 as one of the seven things detestable to God. Pride manifests itself in these forms: arrogance, conceit, self-importance, egotism, vanity, haughty eyes, condescension, scorn, disrespect, snootiness, loftiness, and contemptuousness. The Lord despises proud actions and attitudes. Here are a few of the many verses that describe how God feels about pride:

- ❖ Pride goes before destruction, a haughty spirit before a fall. (Proverbs 16:18)

- ❖ God opposes the proud but gives grace to the humble. (James 4:6)

- ❖ The Lord detests all the proud of heart. Be sure of this: They will not go unpunished. (Proverbs 16:5)

- ❖ Though the Lord is on high, He looks upon the lowly, but the proud He knows from afar. (Psalm 138:6)

If you are not hearing God's voice, you may want to perform a pride inventory in your spirit. Do you practice humility and selflessness, or are you responsible for behaviors that are detestable to God? The verses above assure us that God will punish the proud of heart, and He doesn't go near individuals who are full of pride. If you hold pride in your heart, confess it and ask God's forgiveness. Get rid of all pride, arrogance, conceit, self-importance, haughtiness, disrespect, loftiness, and condescension before you seek the Lord to listen to His voice. Treat others as more important than yourself. Assume the position of the lowly, the meek, and the servant. Don't take it to the extreme so that you resemble a doormat, but approaching the Lord with a contrite heart, in humility, opens the door to receiving God's words of grace, encouragement, and wisdom.

Unfortunately, pride comes much too naturally to all of us, including me. Read about the fall of humankind in Genesis 3. From the very beginning of time, self-importance snuck into human desire. Satan tempted Eve with the idea that she could be all-knowing and wise, like God, if she ate the fruit from the forbidden tree. Deceived by the devil, Eve ate some and gave some to Adam. Pride initiated a sinful response when the evil one presented his temptation.

The need for independence and superiority continues to be the cause of some of our sin today. Proverbs 16:18 says, "Pride goes before destruction, a haughty spirit before a fall." The truth of this verse rang loudly in the Garden of Eden. It still rings true thousands of years later.

Another example of haughtiness is found in Ezekiel 28, the prophecy against the king of Tyre. In verse 17, the Sovereign Lord says, "Your heart became proud on account of your beauty, and you corrupted your wisdom because of your splendor. So I threw you to the earth; I made a spectacle of you before kings." God detested his arrogance. The king's pride preceded his destruction.

In Proverbs 8:13, the wise Solomon says, "To fear the Lord is to hate evil; I hate pride and arrogance, evil behavior and perverse speech." Fear in this case is the same reverence for the Lord that we talked about in the previous chapter. When you respect the Lord, you will detest all pride and arrogance, as He does. Yet arrogance sneaks into all areas of life. Recall that pride inventory we talked about? It may be necessary to make that assessment daily, even hourly.

If pride in any form resides in your life, don't expect to be close to God and hear from Him regularly. Psalm 138:6 says, "Though the Lord is on high, He looks upon the lowly, but the proud He knows from afar." As another passage I've already quoted says,

"God opposes the proud but gives grace to the humble. Submit yourselves, then, to God. Resist the devil, and he will flee from you. Come near to God and He will come near to you" (James 4:6-8). God spends time with humble people who submit themselves to Him and make time for Him. God distances Himself from the self-righteous, prideful, judgmental person.

When the needle on the pride-o-meter registers anywhere on the gauge, take action immediately to dispose of all forms of pride. Humble yourself before the Lord. Submit yourself to Him and exalt Him, rather than yourself. Show the Lord how much you trust in Him for everything. Relinquish your control to the Most High. Place the desires of others ahead of your own. Do not judge any person or behavior. Assume the servant position in God's kingdom.

Do you struggle with judging others or promoting yourself to a higher pedestal? What alerts you of your arrogance? I can tell you truly, when I do not practice the humility of a servant, I should not expect God will speak to me. No matter my standing or position in the world, I am but an unworthy sinner, forgiven and saved by God's grace alone. I am no better than anyone else. If I do not treat others better than myself, God has no business with me, and therefore no reason to talk to me. Anytime I have seated myself on the judgment throne with regard to another human being, God has given me an opportunity to experience the same affliction, position, or experience as the one I judged. Very soon I've gained a new appreciation and respect for the one I condemned because I have walked down a similar path. Becoming the object of my own pride rapidly and effectively cuts me down to size. When the roadblock of pride comes down, my reception of God's voice dramatically improves.

The Bible provides many significant illustrations of humility. Jesus, God's own Son, displayed the ultimate humility when He left His throne in heaven and came to earth to be the sacrificial Lamb and die for our sins. Another dramatic demonstration of Christ's servanthood took place when He washed the feet of His disciples. We can imitate this kind of humility when we selflessly serve our own subordinates, or, better yet, those we judge. This foot washing can be accomplished literally or figuratively. Think of a way you might take an unassuming position with someone you lead, manage, or influence. Is there any type of metaphorical foot washing you could perform for him or her? Maybe picking up a towel and basin of water is what you really need.

Let's examine the enemy's deceit in our thoughts, which gives birth to overconfidence.

LIE #1: I can take care of myself. I know what's best for me.

I look back at all those months and years I spent in midlife depression, feeling lonely and empty inside. I didn't know how I could feel this way when I had built a full life for myself. I'd married a wonderful man and had two beautiful children. We lived in a decent home in a nice neighborhood. We both had decent jobs. I followed Jesus and served in ministries at church. My children participated in sports and other activities. We spent time with our friends. We took nice vacations. I had a good life. Still, something inside made me hope and believe there had to be more to life than what I was experiencing. The full life I had created for myself left me feeling empty and alone. I had a crazy, busy existence that left me no time to spend alone with God—no room for true joy and peace that can be found only in a relationship with Jesus Christ.

God allowed me to hit rock bottom in my depression so that I had nowhere to turn but to Him. He had to use something to get my attention. He wanted me to experience more of Him so I would understand the depth of His love for me and trust Him with all my heart. I exude gratitude as I reminisce about how God worked through my depression counselor to fascinate me with a new and exciting relationship with Him. Every penny I invested in counseling returned great riches as I received mentoring on how to get close to God by listening to His voice. It's priceless!

As I sought Jesus and took time to build a relationship with Him, He honored my effort by making His presence known to me. We may not always feel His presence, but He's always there within us. We just have to ask Him to show Himself to us and then be open to experience Jesus however He chooses to manifest His presence in our lives. Christ reveals and expresses Himself in numerous fashions: in our thoughts; through dreams and visions; with spiritual impressions and promptings; through song lyrics, books, and movies; by way of other people; and most obviously through Scripture.

The first time I heard God's voice remains the most powerful, most meaningful moment of my existence. When the God of the universe chose to speak to me, an ordinary human being, it changed my life forever! When I knew I had heard God's voice once, I desired to hear it again and again. I eagerly made time to be with God every day. I did whatever was required to meet with God and listen to what He would say to me. It became my new reason to live—my new purpose in life.

I started by going to Jesus with my problems; it was all about me. I would take problem after problem to Him and ask for His wisdom and guidance for all of life's circumstances. God helped me get through the challenges each new day brought, and my focus shifted from what He could do for me to what I could do for Him. When I was a mess on the inside, I could not be used effectively by God. As I allowed Him to work in me, He changed major things in my life. Over a couple years' time, He completely transformed the crazy, busy schedule I had created for myself to the life of peace He wanted me to experience. My *good* life did not equate with God's *best* for me. The full life that Jesus came to give me far exceeds any life I could design for myself. It turns out I didn't know what was best for me, but God did. When I relinquished control of my life to Him, He led me down the path He marked out for me.

TRUTH #1: God will take care of you. He knows what's best for you.

God's ways are higher than our ways. He knows what's best for us. He has a purpose for creating us and a plan for our lives that is better than any plans we design. That's why He desires that we trust Him and depend on Him for everything. When I ran ahead on my own, creating a full life for myself, eventually I fell flat on my face. However, when I surrendered my control to God and submitted myself to Him, He slowly and carefully disassembled the life I had built for myself and rebuilt it with Jesus Christ at the center. As a result, He enabled me to do the good works He had prepared in advance for me to do.

The Truth in God's Word:

Seek the Lord while He may found; call on Him while He is near. Let the wicked forsake his way and the evil man his thoughts. Let him turn to the Lord, and He will have mercy on him, and to our God, for He will freely pardon. "For My thoughts are not your thoughts, neither are your ways My ways," declares the Lord. "As the heavens are higher than the earth, so are My ways higher than your ways and My thoughts than your thoughts. As the rain and the snow come down from heaven, and do not return to it without watering the earth and making it bud and flourish, so that it yields seed for the sower and bread for the eater, so is My word that goes out from My mouth: It will not return to Me empty, but will accomplish what I desire and achieve the purpose for which I sent it." (Isaiah 55:6-11)

"For I know the plans I have for you," declares the Lord, "plans to prosper you and not to harm you, plans to give you hope and a future. Then you will call upon Me and come and pray to Me, and I will listen to you. You will seek Me and find Me when you seek Me with all your heart. I will be found by you," declares the Lord. (Jeremiah 29:11-14)

The Lord will fulfill His purpose for me; Your love, O Lord, endures forever—do not abandon the works of Your hands. (Psalm 138:8)

All the days ordained for me were written in Your book before one of them came to be. (Psalm 139:16)

For we are God's workmanship, created in Christ Jesus to do good works, which God prepared in advance for us to do. (Ephesians 2:10)

LIE #2: I am in control of my own life.

It took a wake-up call like depression to make me aware that I was not in control of my own life at all. While battling the gloominess, my great life quickly crumbled around me. I had no strength or desire to live it or carry out my best-laid plans. In fact, I had no power over my emotions, my mental state, or my physical condition. Tears ran down my cheeks for no apparent reason. My mind could not concentrate long enough to accomplish a task. My short-term memory failed regularly. Insomnia robbed me of sleep. Anger replaced patience and tolerance. Confusion prevailed over clarity and focus. Happiness was exchanged with sadness and indifference. In essence, life as I knew it existed no more. I became the opposite of my normal. Unfortunately, all this was necessary to help me understand one major truth: I am not in control of my own life—God is, and I am completely dependent on Him for everything. Is your life rock solid? May I suggest that if you have not built your life on the Rock, trusting fully in Jesus Christ, what seems solid could very well disintegrate before your eyes?

TRUTH #2: Christ controls all things.

Paul said it best in Ephesians 1:17-22:

> I keep asking that the God of our Lord Jesus Christ, the glorious Father, may give you the Spirit of wisdom and revelation, so that you may know Him better. I pray also that the eyes of your heart may be enlightened in order that you may know the hope to which He has called you, the riches of His glorious inheritance in the saints, and His incomparably great power for us who believe. That power is like the working of His mighty strength, which He exerted in Christ when He raised Him from the dead and seated Him at His right hand in the heavenly realms, far above all rule and authority, power and dominion, and every title that can be given, not only in the present age but also in the one to come. And God

placed all things under His feet and appointed Him to be head over everything for the church, which is His body, the fullness of Him Who fills everything in every way.

Another verse that sheds light on God's omnipotence is Psalm 103:19, "The Lord has established His throne in heaven, and His kingdom rules over all."

Ironically, the devil exerts effort to control us by filling our minds with misconceptions and false beliefs. It seems when we buy into these lies, we give our control to him. However, the truth is that God is in control of all things—He controls Satan's attempts at controlling us. Say that fast five times.

God does not allow anything to happen to us without His permission. We see this illustrated in the story of Job. God allowed Satan to test Job, but only within His control. "The Lord said to Satan, 'Very well, then, everything he [Job] has is in your hands, but on the man himself do not lay a finger'" (Job 1:12). At that, Satan began the process of removing everything from Job's life and livelihood, including seven thousand sheep, three thousand camels, five hundred yoke of oxen, five hundred donkeys, a large number of servants, seven sons, and three daughters. Even after this, Job fell to the ground and worshipped God.

Next, Satan reasoned with God to inflict harm on Job's body. "The Lord said to Satan, 'Very well, then, he is in your hands; but you must spare his life'" (Job 2:6). So Satan afflicted Job with painful sores all over his body. Even Job's wife advised him to "Curse God and die!" (Job 2:9). But still, Job did not sin.

God allows us to be tested and tempted, but never beyond what we can withstand. "No temptation has seized you except what is common to man. And God is faithful; He will not let you be tempted beyond what you can bear. But when you are tempted, He will also provide a way out so that you can stand up under it" (1 Corinthians 10:13). The way out is to draw on the power of the Holy Spirit, the same power that raised Jesus from the dead. This kind of power strengthens us and enables us to bear up under extreme circumstances. The God Who is in control of the universe dwells in you!

The Truth in God's Word:

And His incomparably great power for us who believe. That power is like the working of His mighty strength, which He exerted in Christ when He raised Him from the dead and seated Him at His right hand in the heavenly realms, far above all rule and authority, power and dominion, and every title that can be given, not only in the present age but also in the one to come. And God placed all things under His feet and appointed Him to be head over everything for the church, which is His body, the fullness of Him Who fills everything in every way. (Ephesians 1:19-22)

God, the blessed and only Ruler, the King of kings and Lord of lords, Who alone is immortal and who lives in unapproachable light, Whom no one has seen or can see. To Him be honor and might forever. Amen. (1 Timothy 6:15-16)

Shout with joy to God, all the earth! Sing to the glory of His name; offer Him glory and praise! Say to God, "How awesome are Your deeds! So great is Your power that Your enemies cringe before You. All the earth bows down to You; they sing praise to You, they sing praise to Your name." Come and see what God has done, how awesome His works in man's behalf! He turned the sea into dry land, they passed through the river on foot—come, let us rejoice in Him. He rules forever by His power, His eyes watch the nations—let not the rebellious rise up against Him. Praise our God, O peoples, let the sound of His praise be heard; He has preserved our lives and kept our feet from slipping. For You, O God, tested us; You refined us like silver. (Psalm 66:1-10)

LIE #3: I am better than ____ because I ____ (Fill in the blanks).

Do any thoughts similar to these ever run through your mind?

I am better than _____ because I...lead a church ministry, read the Bible every day, pray faithfully, go to church every Sunday, etc.

I am better than _____ because I have children who are...good students, well-behaved, not rebellious, good athletes, solid Christians, etc.

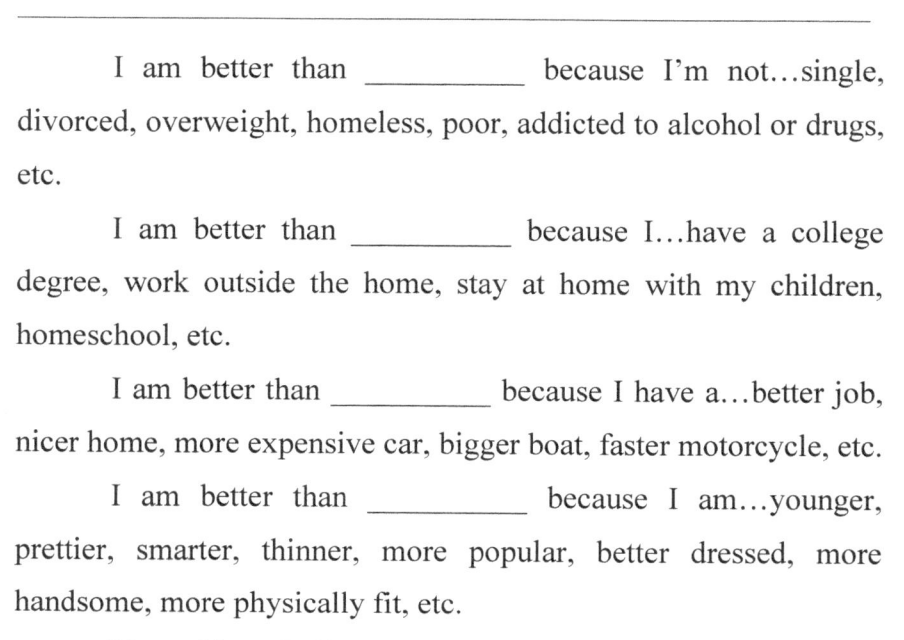

I am better than _____ because I'm not…single, divorced, overweight, homeless, poor, addicted to alcohol or drugs, etc.

I am better than _____ because I…have a college degree, work outside the home, stay at home with my children, homeschool, etc.

I am better than _____ because I have a…better job, nicer home, more expensive car, bigger boat, faster motorcycle, etc.

I am better than _____ because I am…younger, prettier, smarter, thinner, more popular, better dressed, more handsome, more physically fit, etc.

If anything similar to these statements rings true for you, pride may be the barrier between you and God.

TRUTH #3: When you exalt yourself, you will be humbled. When you humble yourself, you will be exalted.

Sometimes God uses difficult circumstances to humble us. Matthew 5:45 says, "He causes His sun to shine on the evil and the good, and sends rain on the righteous and the unrighteous." This verse implies that God allows good things to happen to both evil people and good people. Also, He allows both Christians and non-Christians to experience storms and trials. Scripture also says when we applaud ourselves, we will be put in our place, but when we act in a respectful, subservient manner, we will be revered and esteemed. In Luke 14:11, Jesus says, "For everyone who exalts himself will be humbled, and he who humbles himself will be exalted." In essence, comparing ourselves to others and elevating ourselves above them is a dangerous, ungodly practice that could plug the communication channel from God to you. When you seek to listen to God's voice, exercise humility, placing Him and others ahead of yourself, and watch the roadblock between you and God fall down.

Jesus Christ modeled the ultimate humility, and therefore God exalted Him to the highest place. Philippians 2:3-11 says,

> Do nothing out of selfish ambition or vain conceit, but in humility consider others better than yourselves. Each of you should look not only to your own interests, but also to the interests of others.
> Your attitude should be the same as that of Christ Jesus:
>
> Who, being in very nature God, did not consider equality with God something to be grasped, but made Himself nothing, taking the very nature of a servant, being made in human likeness. And being found in appearance as a man, He humbled Himself and became obedient to death—even death on a cross! Therefore God exalted Him to the highest place and gave Him the name that is above every name, that at the name of Jesus every knee should bow, in heaven and on earth and under the earth, and every tongue confess that Jesus Christ is Lord, to the glory of God the Father.

If our God and Creator can humble Himself by coming to earth in the form of a man to serve those who should be serving Him, I think I can humble myself in order to exalt Him high above the heavens and the earth. Considering the interests of others ahead of my own gives glory to God. When God is glorified, He is pleased, and when He is pleased, it is His pleasure to speak to us.

The Truth in God's Word:

"Do not judge, and you will not be judged. Do not condemn, and you will not be condemned. Forgive and you will be forgiven. Give, and it will be given to you. A good measure, pressed down, shaken together and running over, will be poured into your lap. For with the measure you use, it will be measured to you." (Luke 6:37-38)

You, therefore, have no excuse, you who pass judgment on someone else, for at whatever point you judge the other, you are condemning yourself, because you who pass judgment do the same things. Now we know that God's judgment against those who do such things is based on truth. So when you, a mere man, pass judgment on them and yet do the same things, do you think you will escape God's judgment? (Romans 2:1-3)

God "will give to each person according to what he has done." (Romans 2:6)

If anyone thinks he is something when he is nothing, he deceives himself. Each one should test his own actions. Then he can take pride in himself, without comparing himself to somebody else, for each one should carry his own load. (Galatians 6:3-4)

We do not dare to classify or compare ourselves with some who commend themselves. When they measure themselves by themselves and compare themselves with themselves, they are not wise. (2 Corinthians 10:12)

This is what the Lord says: "Let not the wise man boast of his wisdom or the strong man boast of his strength or the rich man boast of his riches, but let him who boasts boast about this: that he understands and knows Me, that I am the Lord, Who exercises kindness, justice and righteousness on earth, for in these I delight," declares the Lord. (Jeremiah 9:23-24)

But, "Let him who boasts boast in the Lord."[8] For it is not the one who commends himself who is approved, but the one whom the Lord commends. (2 Corinthians 10:17-18)

Listen to God's heart about pride in His Word and His communications to me in the following *Manna for Today* excerpts.

---

[8] Jeremiah 9:24

The end of a matter is better than its beginning, and patience is better than pride. Do not be quickly provoked in your spirit, for anger resides in the lap of fools (Ecclesiastes 7:8-9).

Patience before Pride[9]

When you find yourself in a difficult situation; be patient and see it through. The end of the matter will always be better than the start, if only because it's the end. Do not let a spirit of anger rise up within you. Anger may cause a person to sin. Rather be tolerant of the situation, and endure it without grumbling and complaining. Patient endurance produces character. The patient will inherit the promises of God.

Do not be arrogant in times of difficulty, but in humility, consider others better than yourself. Do not hold onto your pride, it will surely lead to destruction. Patiently wait upon the Lord. Serve Him in good times and bad. Be patient in hope, it will be an anchor for your soul, and get you through the long days before you.

Put your faith and trust in Me alone. I am in control of all things, and have My best in mind for you. My time table is different from yours. My days seem like years to you, and My hours seem like weeks. Before you realize it, you will have reached the end of the suffering. Approach each matter with patience, and in the end, you will be rewarded.

Patient perseverance produces moral fiber. Practicing patience is a step in your sanctification process. As you practice patience, you become more and more like Christ. Subject yourself to the Spirit of God within you, and I, Myself, will sanctify you through and through. You are not your own. You have been sanctified in Christ. Through His death, you are reconciled to Me. Be patient in your suffering. I will see you through. When you have reached the end, you will look back and say, "With God's help I made it through." Now claim the promises I give you. Your inheritance unfolds before you—a life of eternity with Me in heaven.

✝

---

[9] Sindy Nagel, "Patience Before Pride" in *Manna for Today: Bread from Heaven for Each Day* (Bloomington, IN: WestBow Press 2012), 68.

But He said to me, "My grace is sufficient for you, for My power is made perfect in weakness." Therefore I will boast all the more gladly about my weaknesses, so that Christ's power may rest on me. That is why, for Christ's sake, I delight in weaknesses, in insults, in hardships, in persecutions, in difficulties. For when I am weak, then I am strong (2 Corinthians 12:9-10).

My Grace is Sufficient for You[10]

My precious child, My favor remains upon you. I bless you with My mercy and loving kindness. My grace is adequate for each difficulty you face. My influence is most dominant when I use an empty, broken vessel. When you are drained, I fill you with My Spirit. I seal you by the power of My Spirit for My good work. My strength pours out of the cracks in your exterior. My power is made great in the midst of your weakness.

If you were flawless, you would have no need of Me. No demonstration of My power is revealed through the self-sufficient one. Be not proud in your independence, but boast with enthusiasm about your weaknesses, and My power will rest on you. Delight in the hardships you face. Your adversity is the window to My authority. The difficulties that challenge you are the perfect opportunities for Me to prove My might. I will work with your imperfections because My power is completed in you.

My grace is sufficient for you. When you trust Me for your strength, I will not leave you in your weakness. I am enough for you. Do not be ashamed to depend on Me. When you lean on Me, I am your rock. When you call to Me, I hear your cry. When your trial is too much for you to bear, I am with you. The thorn in your side may torment you, but My power is made perfect in weakness. My grace is enough for you to remain strong. The trials you walk through bring you closer to Me. Have faith in Me, and I will carry you through. Rely on Me alone for your strength. My might shows through your helplessness. My grace is sufficient for you. Trust in My omnipotence. I am unstoppable.

✝

---

[10] Sindy Nagel, "My Grace is Sufficient for You" in *Manna for Today: Bread from Heaven for Each Day* (Bloomington, IN: WestBow Press 2012), 89.

Those who trust in the Lord are like Mount Zion, which cannot be shaken but endures forever (Psalm 125:1).

Like a Mountain[11]

My blessed one, when you trust in Me, you are like a mountain that cannot be shaken. You are like Mount Zion, which lasts forever. Put your trust in Me, and you will not be traumatized by anything that comes your way. The element of surprise will not frighten you when you depend on the Lord. Earthquakes will come and go, but your foundation will remain strong and intact. Waves may crash against you, but your surface will not be eroded by them.

Does it feel awkward to trust in Me completely? Do you find it difficult to relinquish your control to Me? Think about this. Do you give over your power to Me or do I give over My power to you? I rule over all things whether you believe it or not. Get rid of the deception that causes you to feel that you have dominance in any situation, except that which I give you. Your dominion over the birds of the air and the fish of the sea was given to you by Me. Humble yourself in the sight of the Lord, for the Lord despises the self-righteous person, but gives grace to the lowly, unassuming one.

Like a mighty mountain, you will not crumble and fall into the sea at the first sign of disaster. You will remain forever in My strength. Your constitution will not waver. Your foundation in Me is sure. Stay true to Me. My love for you endures all things. My power is immeasurable. I protect you and keep you from evil. I provide you with everything you need. I have your well-being in mind. I know the future. You are safe with Me. I am steadfast. My love is unconditional. I will never fail you. You can depend on Me. I am like a mighty mountain. I will not be shaken. I will not fall. I will outlast everything on this earth.

✝

---

[11]Sindy Nagel, "Like a Mountain" in *Manna for Today: Bread from Heaven for Each Day* (Bloomington, IN: WestBow Press 2012), 93.

Self-Reflection:

1. On a scale from 0 to 4, rate yourself on the frequency these characteristics are displayed in your life: 0=Never, 1=Rarely, 2=Seldom, 3=Regularly, 4=Too Often

   a. Arrogance _____
   b. Conceit _____
   c. Self-importance _____
   d. Ego _____
   e. Vanity _____
   f. Haughtiness _____
   g. Condescension _____
   h. Scorn _____
   i. Disrespect _____
   j. Snootiness _____
   k. Loftiness _____
   l. Contemptuousness _____

2. Identify three ways you could try to eliminate the above traits you identify with.

3. Think of a recent example when you treated someone disrespectfully, and record it here. Now describe how you could have handled that situation with more humility.

4. In what circumstances have you acted independently without seeking God's will, wisdom, or guidance?

5. How might those situations have played out differently had you consulted God before you acted?

6. To whom have you compared yourself lately? Or whom have you judged unfairly? In what ways?

7. Name someone you have compared yourself to and concluded that you don't measure up to him or her. Is that a result of your humility or your insecurity? Explain your answer.

Removing the Barrier of Pride

Ask God to expose the lies and help you identify any false beliefs that cause a barrier of pride between you and God. Record them here.

Request that God bring memories to your mind of His presence in your life as it relates to your struggles with pride. Pay close attention to what He is doing and saying to you in your thoughts. Write it down here.

Allow the Holy Spirit to lead you to Scripture verses that shine the light of God's truth into the deceptions you've believed. The concordance in your Bible comes in handy when you're searching for verses regarding a topic or word you hear from the Lord. Write the Bible verses and references here.

In the power given to you by Jesus Christ, through the shedding of His blood, take authority over the enemy and his attempts to distract and confuse you with his misconceptions. Speak out loud to rebuke the devil and proclaim the truth of God's Word, which you recorded above.

Pray:

Almighty God, thank You for loving me and desiring a relationship with me despite my prideful ways. Please forgive me for acting in a manner that is detestable to You. I lay down all arrogance, pride, conceit, and self-righteousness at Your feet, Lord. I trade in my haughty spirit for a spirit of humility and submission. I will try not to pass judgment on others, nor put myself on a pedestal above anyone else. Help me listen to and obey the direction of Your Holy Spirit as He guides me to adopt the heart of a servant and strive to act more like Jesus. I lift You up as the Sovereign Lord, Who rules over everything on earth and in heaven. Father, please help me to seek You for direction in everything I do and put Your desires and the interests of others ahead of my own. I cannot do any of this on my own without the power and strength of Jesus Christ. Please grant me the ability and the blessing of hearing Your voice. I ask all this in Jesus' name. Amen.

Listen:

Lord, what do You want me to know about my pride? (Write down all your thoughts and identify which thoughts may actually be God's voice.)

Chapter 4

Worry
The Enemy of Trust

"Therefore, I tell you, do not worry about your life, what you will eat or drink; or about your body, what you will wear. Is not life more important than food, and the body more important than clothes?" (Matthew 6:25)

The sovereign cure for worry is prayer.—William James

From God's Heart to Yours

Fretful one, I understand your anxiousness. It is difficult for you to trust fully in Me. You may have a good reason not to trust in humanity; you've been let down in the past. You may suppress all expectations when dealing with your friends and family. However, I am your Abba, your faithful Daddy. I never leave you or forget you. I provide all your needs. I keep My promises. I know what's best for you. I hear your prayers and answer them according to My perfect will.

Life is more important than food; feast on My words. The body is more important than apparel; clothe yourself in humility and love. Worry will not add one hour to your life. But seek first My kingdom and My righteousness, and I will provide all these things for you. I know what you need to survive, and I know what you need to thrive. Both shall be yours when you depend on Me.

Do not worry about tomorrow. Exercise your faith by trusting wholeheartedly in Me. Knowing Me more intimately will increase your confidence in Me. Spend time in My Word and listen to My voice. Learn about My character and rely on My abilities. Be sure of what you hope for and certain of what you do not see. Your foundation will be secure when you build your faith in Me. I am your Rock; I do not change. I am the same yesterday, today, and forever. I will not disappoint you. I am the Giver of all good gifts. Are you ready to receive them?

WORRY

Worry does not add anything to our lives; in fact, it sucks the life right out of us. Worry equals not trusting fully in God. When we don't trust God for everything, we distance ourselves from Him. Not relying completely on God to care for us, protect us, and provide for us, we detach ourselves from Him and His enormous power. God is omniscient: He knows our every need. God is omnipotent: He is the almighty, all-powerful, invincible Lord. God is omnipresent: He never leaves us; He's always with us. God is the All-Sufficient One: He is enough. God is trustworthy: He will do what He promises.

God does not ask us to have blind faith and complete trust in a human being. He does ask us to put our trust and confidence in Him alone. We can rest in the assurance that He will take care of us. He is the Most High God. He is dependable, reliable, and faithful.

Jesus said, "Therefore I tell you, do not worry about your life, what you will eat or drink; or about your body, what you will wear. Is not life more important than food, and the body more important than clothes? ...Who of you by worrying can add a single hour to his life?" (Matthew 6:25, 27). Proverbs 3:5-6 says, "Trust in the Lord with all your heart and lean not on your own understanding; in all your ways acknowledge Him, and He will make your paths straight." God wants us to be completely dependent on Him for everything.

Not depending on God and trusting in Him completely may put distance between Him and you.

God loves children and speaks to them. Perhaps He does so because children are more dependent. Are you approaching God as a child? Are you dependent on Him? Remember the story of the boy Samuel? After God had spoken to him, Samuel didn't question God; he listened and obeyed. (See 1 Samuel 3 for the whole story.) God spoke to the boy because he practiced humility and willingly served the Lord. He did not have preconceived ideas about how God would talk to him. Samuel did not practice the freedom of self-sufficiency. He enthusiastically listened to God however God chose to speak to him, and then he obeyed.

This story offers encouragement. God speaks to people of all ages and all spiritual maturity levels. He doesn't stop calling you just because you don't recognize Him. He keeps pursuing you until you learn the sound of His voice. He will speak to you when you are still and ready to listen. Hearing Him is not enough. God looks for people who are dependent on Him, ready to listen to and obey Him. When we practice our independence and do what we please, God may choose not to speak to us. Depending on God and obeying His lead will keep the doors of communication open between you and the Lord.

To hear God's voice, you must become like a child: humble, with a simple faith and reverence for the Lord. In Matthew 18:3, Jesus says, "I tell you the truth, unless you change and become like little children, you will never enter the kingdom of heaven. Therefore, whoever humbles himself like this child is the greatest in the kingdom of heaven." In Mark 10:15, Jesus says, "I tell you the truth, anyone who will not receive the kingdom of God like a little child will never enter it."

Become like a child and surrender to the work and power of the Holy Spirit within you. Trust God, and depend on Him for everything. Walk in submission to God by being sensitive to the voice of the Holy Spirit and acting in obedience to His instruction.

Trusting in the Lord, rather than in ourselves and others, proves to be the most stress-free way to live. Giving our cares over to God, Who controls all things, prevents us from being stifled in our spiritual growth by depending on our own limited understanding. Put your trust in God today, and acknowledge His supreme influence, power, and authority in your life. Permit yourself to relinquish all control and worry to the One who rules and reigns over everything on earth and in heaven. Trade in the following lies for the truth in God's Word.

LIE #1: God won't provide for all my needs.

Independence vs. trust in God—which side of the scale weighs heavier for you? One voice in your head may whisper, *Dependence shows weakness*, while the other voice says, *Do not be anxious about anything. I will take care of all your needs.* Which voice do you listen to? Some of us may hear the voice of our parents: *I raised you to be self-sufficient.*

All our lives, most of us are groomed to be independent individuals. A parent's role is to nurture and train their children to be self-sufficient and self-reliant. When we were babies, our parents taught us to soothe ourselves by letting us cry. Our mothers weaned us from the breast or bottle so we would not remain dependent on that source of nourishment. They potty-trained us to rid us of our dependence on diapers. When we were toddlers, they encouraged us to feed and dress ourselves. Socialization skills were achieved through daycare, pre-school, sports, church, and other extracurricular activities. Our parents gave us opportunities to be away from them by leaving us with friends or babysitters. Before we knew it, they were teaching us to drive our way to independence, and in another breath or two, we left the nest for college or a career. Building confidence in children to make it on their own is what parents do.

Dependence is often perceived as weakness. None of us wants to appear weak or fragile. Contrary to the ways of the world, however, God desires that His children remain dependent on Him and trust Him to meet all our needs. In Luke 18:16-17, Jesus says, "Let the little children come to Me, and do not hinder them, for the kingdom of God belongs to such as these. I tell you the truth, anyone who will not receive the kingdom of God like a little child will never enter it." In this passage, the term *little children* literally means *"babes"*[12] It refers to infants who depend on their caregiver for *everything*. That's how God wants us to relate to Him—depending on Him for all our needs.

When life brings us circumstances that require us to be dependent on another person for anything, we become anxious and proud about asking for assistance or receiving support. To rely on someone else to meet our needs is counterintuitive to our culture. So often, our life experiences teach us that no one is worthy of our trust. It seems at times even God is as unreliable as our human counterparts. He knows our needs but may not meet them in our timeframe in the manner we expect. But that doesn't mean He isn't trustworthy. It may mean:

- ❖ He sees the bigger picture; His ways are higher than ours; He knows best.

- ❖ In all things He works for the good of those who love Him (see Romans 8:28).

- ❖ Our perceived needs are really more like desires.

- ❖ He's teaching us faith, patience, trust, character, and/or perseverance.

- ❖ He has given us free will and does not desire to control our choices at this time.

---

[12] Jamieson, R., Fausset, A. R., & Brown, D., *Commentary Critical and Explanatory on the Whole Bible* (Oak Harbor, WA: Logos Research Systems, Inc. 1997), Vol. 2, p. 118.

We strive to live the lyrics of the old Frank Sinatra song, "I did it *my* way." Control is not easy to relinquish. Trusting another human being to meet our expectations is even more difficult. However, God does not ask us to trust in people, who will most surely let us down at some point. Rather, He desires we trust in Him alone. When He doesn't answer our prayers in our time frame or in line with our expectations, though, we unfairly throw God into the untrustworthy pool.

TRUTH #1: God will meet all your needs.

The truth is…God *will* meet all your needs. The question is, what do you really need? Your ideas may consist of an entirely different list than what God determines you need. Too often we set our sights on lavish things, but God is more concerned about the needs of our hearts. When we delight ourselves in the Lord, making our relationship with Him our first priority, He will give us the desires of our hearts (see Psalm 37:4). Even this verse can be misconstrued. Some may feel this verse implies that God will give us everything we want. However, I interpret this verse to mean that God will place in our hearts the wholesome, healthy desires He wants us to feed on. When we allow God access to our souls, He gives us what we stand in need of. When we give Him our time, He honors our time with His presence, provision, peace, and wisdom. Our needs may be met in ways we never dreamed possible.

In Philippians 4:10-13, Paul expressed his thankfulness for gifts given to him by the body of Christ at Philippi. He shared with them that he had learned to be content in all circumstances. He knew how it felt to be in need, and he knew what it was to have plenty, to be well fed or hungry, in feast or famine. He could do everything through Christ, Who gave him strength.

Read the story in Matthew 6:25-34, where Jesus instructs His disciples and followers not to worry about their life, what they would eat or drink, or their body and what they would wear. He reassures them that God takes care of the birds of the air and the lilies of the field, and His children are much more valuable. The Lord knows our needs, and we should not waste a minute worrying about them. In summary, Jesus taught, "But seek first His kingdom and His righteousness, and all these things will be given to you as well. Therefore, do not worry about tomorrow, for tomorrow will worry about itself. Each day has enough trouble of its own" (Matthew 6:33-34). Can I hear an "Amen"?

Will God meet your needs? Of course He will. His Word declares it, and He keeps His promises. But what do you really need? Compare your list to God's.

The Truth in God's Word:

And my God will meet all your needs according to His glorious riches in Christ Jesus. (Philippians 4:19)

"And when you pray, do not keep on babbling like pagans, for they think they will be heard because of their many words. Do not be like them, for your Father knows what you need before you ask Him." (Matthew 6:7-8)

The Lord will guide you always; He will satisfy your needs in a sun-scorched land and will strengthen your frame. You will be like a well-watered garden, like a spring whose waters never fail. (Isaiah 58:11)

"So I say to you: Ask and it will be given to you; seek and you will find; knock and the door will be opened to you. For everyone who asks receives; he who seeks finds; and to him who knocks, the door will be opened. Which of you fathers, if your son asks for a fish, will give him a snake instead? Or if he asks for an egg, will give him a scorpion? If you then though you are evil, know how to give good gifts to your children, how much more will your Father in heaven give the Holy Spirit to those who ask Him!" (Luke 11:9-13)

Delight yourself in the Lord and He will give you the desires of your heart. Commit your way to the Lord; trust in Him and He will do this: He will make your righteousness shine like the dawn, the justice of your cause like the noonday sun. (Psalm 37:4-6)

"But seek first His kingdom and His righteousness, and all these things will be given to you as well. Therefore, do not worry about tomorrow, for tomorrow will worry about itself. Each day has enough trouble of its own." (Matthew 6:33-34)

[LIE] #2: I can't trust God because He let me down in the past.

Is this a familiar voice in your head? *Where is God now? He didn't answer my prayers last time. Why should I trust Him this time?* When the trials and storms of life come with a vengeance, it's easy for a Christ follower to wonder whether God is truly trustworthy and to ask these questions:

- Where is God in all of this?
- Why isn't God protecting me from this struggle?
- Why is God allowing me to go through this difficulty?
- Why did God allow that illness to take that person from me?
- If God is so good, why would He allow this to happen?

Ultimately, you'll have to seek God and His Word for the answers to these questions. If, or how, God answers you is completely at His discretion. He may choose to let you in on His plans for you; He may disclose just enough information for the step you currently stand on; or He may decide it's best not to tell you anything at the moment. But you still can ask; He'd love to have this conversation with you.

TRUTH #2: God is trustworthy; He never leaves you or forgets you.

In my thirty-five years as a Christian, the last fifteen hearing God's voice, I've discovered that God is trustworthy; however, He allows me to go through difficult times for any or all of these reasons:

- ❖ To bring me into a closer relationship with Him

- ❖ To cause me to trust in Him and depend on Him more fully

- ❖ To teach me a spiritual precept, such as faith, patience, self-control, or mercy

- ❖ To help me relate to someone else who has suffered or will suffer a similar trial

- ❖ To prune me and mature me in my faith journey

Of course, I am not this clear-minded in the midst of the battle. However, after I've walked through the fire, I more fully appreciate that it took the intense heat to refine me into the valuable piece of art that God personally hand-sculpted. I begin to realize why God allowed it, and I see the spiritual growth that occurred as a result of the test. Sometimes I even get to the point of expressing my gratitude to God for the trial, because it changed my life.

Some trials happen for which we may never know or understand God's will or plan. Not only do we question the reason for our trials, but it's easy to feel like God abandons us in our time of need. I can assure you that God is with you wherever you go because His Spirit lives in your heart. You may not *feel* the presence of the Lord, but that doesn't mean He's not with you. When God determines, instructs, calls, ordains, or anoints His people for a certain task, path, process, or trial, He does not allow them to go it alone. He walks the designated path with them, even carrying them at times.

God allows us to suffer trials in order to bring us into a closer relationship with Him. As I've already expressed, during my mid-thirties I battled through a few bouts with depression. The first one caught me off guard. I knew nothing about depression or its symptoms. Five months in a downward spiral passed before I understood and admitted that clinical depression had its grip on me. Antidepressant medication and months of Christian counseling, in addition to time alone with a loving God, saw me through. My relationship with God grew stronger and more personal as I learned to be more dependent on Him to get me through each day.

During my second bout with depression, my anger brewed toward God for letting me endure this kind of trial again. But I found, as the common phrase says, God can handle our anger. I spent a few mornings expressing my anger toward Him and my disappointment in Him. He assured me that it was necessary for me to struggle with this condition again because He had more to teach me, and it was during these trials that He had my full attention and my strong will was most pliable.

Counseling had proven beneficial during the first depression, so I made more counseling appointments the next time. This was no accident—God used my counselor and talk therapy as the venue to perform His healing work in me.

My counselor had just been through a time of spiritual awakening himself. Rather than executing the usual psychotherapy, he shared with me about his freshly deepened relationship with Jesus Christ. He conveyed his recent experiences of listening to God's voice. He described pursuing God as a type of adventure that sounded very exciting and fulfilling. It gave me a new hope and direction in life. It was exactly what I needed to hear.

The counselor gave me a suggested reading list of books written by authors John Eldredge and Stasi Eldredge: *Wild at Heart, Waking the Dead,* and *Captivating.* God used these books to awaken my heart as the authors described what they had learned about having a more invigorating relationship with Jesus Christ. They propelled me into seeking the kind of intimate relationship with Christ that He desires with each of His children. My heart began to come alive.

Next I read *Do You Think I'm Beautiful?* by Angela Thomas. She described her relationship with the Lord as a dance. That sounded appealing to me. I began to think of my new relationship with Jesus Christ as a dance. In real life, I had two left feet and no coordination or rhythm. But with Christ as my dance partner, I would become the next Ginger Rogers.

Excitedly, I thought about where He might lead me in the dance of my life. That was the key—I had to let Jesus lead the dance. With His strong arm around my back, He would determine and guide each move I made, and it would be executed very gracefully.

My counseling sessions turned into spiritual mentoring meetings. My counselor described how he listened to God's voice and encouraged me to try it. He instructed me to record my conversations with God in a journal. If not for the depression, the counseling, the books, and the encouragement to listen to God, would I ever have learned to hear His voice? This trial not only saved my emotional and spiritual life, but God used it to transform my life! I am eternally grateful!

The Truth in God's Word:

"I will never leave you or forsake you." (Joshua 1:5)

"Have I not commanded you? Be strong and courageous. Do not be terrified; do not be discouraged, for the Lord your God will be with you wherever you go." (Joshua 1:9)

"Do not let your hearts be troubled. Trust in God; trust also in Me." (John 14:1)

O Sovereign Lord, You are God! Your words are trustworthy, and You have given this good promise to Your servant. Now be pleased to bless the house of Your servant, that it may continue forever in Your sight; for You, O Sovereign Lord, have spoken, and with Your blessing the house of Your servant will be blessed forever. (2 Samuel 7:28-29).

The Lord is a refuge for the oppressed, a stronghold in times of trouble. Those who know Your name will trust in You, for You, Lord, have never forsaken those who seek You. (Psalm 9:9-10)

[LIE]
#3: I need to take care of things myself because God isn't.

Fast food, overnight delivery, express mail, one-hour photo service, instant messaging, Snapchat, 24-hour pharmacy, ATMs, immediate credit approval, mobile deposits, red-eye flights, and instant oatmeal. We want what we want, and we want it right now. Patience is a rare asset in the U.S.A. these days.

Many times it seems God doesn't take care of things the way we would like to see Him do, in the time frame we expect. However, being an omniscient God, He knows everything. He sees the grand picture. He knows and sees things we don't. He wrote the script of our lives before we were conceived. He created us to love us. Why wouldn't we trust Him? Why wouldn't we wait on Him? He deserves our trust. Why do we have to be in control of everything? He's earned our respect.

TRUTH #3: God works all things together for your good.

In our finite minds, we have no idea what our boundless God can do. We cannot comprehend the idea of a God who is omniscient—He knows everything. We don't even know how much we don't know. He sees all and knows all—past, present, and forever into the future. He is limitless—everywhere at all times—omnipresent. God's ways are higher than our ways, His thoughts higher than our thoughts, and His plans and timing are always perfect (see Isaiah 55:9 and Psalm 18:30). He is the omnipotent—all-powerful—Creator of the universe. He never changes: He is the same yesterday, today, and forever (see Hebrews 13:8). He never leaves us or forgets us (see Joshua 1:5). He knows what's best for us, and in all things, He works for the good of those who love Him (see Romans 8:28). The Lord is faithful to all His promises and loving toward all He has made (see Psalm 145:13). What an amazing, awesome Deity we worship!

The Truth in God's Word:

When anxiety was great within me, Your consolation brought joy to my soul. (Psalm 94:19)

An anxious heart weighs a man down, but a kind word cheers him up. (Proverbs 12:25)

Do not be anxious about anything, but in everything, by prayer and petition, with thanksgiving, present your requests to God. And the peace of God, which transcends all understanding, will guard your hearts and your minds in Christ Jesus. (Philippians 4:6-7)

Jesus said to His disciples: "Therefore I tell you, do not worry about your life, what you will eat or drink; or about your body, what you will wear. Is not life more important than food, and the body more important than clothes? Look at the birds of the air; they do not sow or reap or store away in barns, and yet your heavenly Father feeds them. Are you not much more valuable than they? Who of you by worrying can add a single hour to his life? And why do you worry about clothes? See how the lilies of the field grow. They do not labor or spin. Yet I tell you that not even Solomon in all his splendor was dressed like one of these. If that is how God clothes the grass of the field, which is here today and tomorrow is thrown into the fire, will He not much more clothe you, O you of little faith? So do not worry, saying, 'What shall we eat?' or 'What shall we drink?' or 'What shall we wear?' For the pagans run after all these things, and your heavenly Father knows that you need them. But seek first His kingdom and His righteousness, and all these things will be given to you as well. Therefore do not worry about tomorrow, for tomorrow will worry about itself. Each day has enough trouble of its own." (Matthew 6:25-34)

Listen to God's heart about worry in His Word and His communications to me in the following *Manna for Today* excerpts.

"Do not let your hearts be troubled. Trust in God; trust also in Me. In My Father's house are many rooms; if it were not so, I would have told you. I am going there to prepare a place for you. And if I go and prepare a place for you, I will come back and take you to be with Me that you also may be where I am. You know the way to the place where I am going" (John 14:1-4).

Trust in God[13]

Do not be concerned about your life after this world. You have entrusted yourself to me. You are using your life to fulfill My purpose in God's kingdom here on earth, but on the day and hour God determines, the life you know now, will come to an end. Do not be anxious; a greater life awaits you. I have gone ahead of you to prepare a place for you in heaven. I will return to you someday, and bring you to the place I have prepared for you. I want you to spend eternity with Me and My Father.

Put your trust in My Father and in Me. My Father's house accommodates many people, but there is only one way to reach My Father's house. I am the way. If you know Me, you know the way to My Father. I am in My Father, and My Father is in Me. Follow Me, and I will lead you to the throne of God, both in this life and in the next. My Father sent Me to do His work. I have accomplished what I was sent to do and returned to My Father's side.

Do not fret about tomorrow. Your tomorrow rests in My hands. Worrying will not add a moment to your life. Cast all your burdens in My direction. Seek My Father before anything else, above all else. He provides everything you ever need or want. My Father's will is set on all good things. Nothing is impossible. Approach God's throne of grace with thanksgiving on your lips. He has fed you, clothed you, and provided you with shelter; but even more than that, He has given you abundant life, even life eternally in His presence. Do not be set in your own ways, but look first to My Father in heaven. He knows all things and has determined what is best for you. He marks the way of the righteous and leads them down His chosen path for His name's sake. Follow His lead. Trust in God completely.

✝

---

[13] Sindy Nagel, "Trust in God" in *Manna for Today: Bread from Heaven for Each Day* (Bloomington, IN: WestBow Press 2012), 88.

Trust in the Lord with all your heart and lean not on your own understanding; in all your ways acknowledge Him and He will make your paths straight (Proverbs 3:5-6).

Trust in Me[14]

My child, the most valuable lessons are learned in "the process." That is true with everything. If I made this all happen for you in a moment, what would you learn from that? You know I can do anything. I can make it happen tomorrow if I choose. There is much for you to know yet. Your growth is part of this process. I may choose to expedite some steps in the process, but you will still experience "the process."

Here is the lesson for now—trust Me. "Trust in Me with all your heart and lean not on your own understanding. In all your ways acknowledge Me and I will make your paths straight" (Proverbs 3:5-6). This is a verse for a lifetime; now live it. Let Me break it down for you.

You need to "trust Me."
You need to "trust Me with all."
You need to "trust Me with all your heart."
You need to "lean."
You need to "lean not on your own."
You need to "lean not on your own understanding."
You need to "acknowledge."
You need to "acknowledge Me."
You need to "acknowledge Me in all."
You need to "acknowledge Me in all your ways."
You need to "acknowledge Me in all your ways and I will."
You need to "acknowledge Me in all your ways and I will make your paths."
You need to "acknowledge Me in all your ways and I will make your paths straight."
You need to "trust in Me with all your heart and lean not on your own understanding; in all your ways acknowledge Me and I will make your paths straight."
You need to.

---

[14] Sindy Nagel, "Trust in Me" in *Manna for Today: Bread from Heaven for Each Day* (Bloomington, IN: WestBow Press 2012), 74.

You need.
You

Understand? It's up to you. It's up to you to trust Me. I am in control. I will not fail you. I will make your paths straight. The shortest distance between two points is a straight line. Trust in Me, and I will make your paths straight; it will be the shortest distance for you to travel in "the process."

He said: "The Lord is my rock, my fortress and my deliverer; my God is my rock, in whom I take refuge, my shield and the horn of my salvation. He is my stronghold, my refuge and my savior—from violent men You save me." (2 Samuel 22:2-3).

Your Rock and Your Refuge[15]

I am your rock and your refuge. I am your stronghold in times of trouble. I am your fortress and your hiding place. When you are in danger, run to Me, and I will protect you. As you face trial and tribulation, I will be your anchor of hope. Cling to Me, and I will hold on to you. Have faith in Me, and I will be your guide. You do not walk alone; I go with you wherever you go. When you face evil, I am on your side. Together we will stand and fight to overcome all forces against you.

Do not worry or be anxious about the future. Cast all your cares upon Me, and I will sustain you. Give your burdens to Me, and in return, I will give you rest. Trade in your anxiety for My perfect peace. A heart at peace gives life to the body. Bask in My peace, and experience true life as I have designed it. Slow down, breathe deeply, and rest in Me. I will carry your load. A life too busy brings discontent. Eliminate the unnecessary, and concentrate on My will. I will show you the most excellent way.

Do not be lazy, but do not labor in vain only to store up a wealth of your own. Be generous with what you have. Give freely, as it has been given to you. Do not put your hope in wealth, which is uncertain; but put your hope in Me, and I will provide you with everything for your enjoyment. I provide water for the thirsty. I provide food for the hungry. I provide rest for the weary and strength for the weak. I provide a way out, when there is no other way. I give you good gifts without cost. Trust in Me, and I will supply you with all you require. Believe in Me, and you will have a life that is full. I am your portion. I am all you need.

✝

---

[15] Sindy Nagel, "Your Rock and Your Refuge" in *Manna for Today: Bread from Heaven for Each Day* (Bloomington, IN: WestBow Press 2012), 130.

Self-Reflection:

1. Place a checkmark next to the things you worry about:

    ___Food
    ___Shelter
    ___Clothing
    ___Social Status
    ___Relationships/Spouse
    ___Children/Grandchildren
    ___Parents
    ___Finances
    ___Job/Career
    ___Appearance/Health
    ___Education
    ___Future

2. List other people, things, or situations that cause you stress, worry, or anxiety:

3. Let's unpack this Scripture passage:

    Do not be anxious about anything, but in everything, by prayer and petition, with thanksgiving, present your requests to God. And the peace of God, which transcends all understanding, will guard your hearts and your minds in Christ Jesus. (Philippians 4:6-7).

    a. What is acceptable to be anxious or worry about?

    b. In what posture or position are we to approach everything?

c. With what attitude are we to present our requests to God?

d. When we approach God with a thankful, trusting heart, what are we promised?

e. What does that gift do for our hearts and minds?

f. When we are at peace by trusting in God, what happens to our worries?

4. How is it possible to experience peace in the middle of life's storms?

5. Next time you begin to feel anxious or fretful about something, what will you do?

6. Identify a situation that you currently face or foresee in the future. Write out a plan to give your worry over to the Lord and trust Him for the outcome.

7. Write out two or three Bible verses that you will memorize and claim the next time you find yourself fretting about anything.

Removing the Barrier of Worry

Ask God to expose the lies and help you identify any false beliefs that cause a barrier of worry between you and God. Record them here.

Request that God bring memories to your mind of His presence in your life as it relates to your struggles with worry. Pay close attention to what He is doing and saying to you in your thoughts. Write it down here.

Allow the Holy Spirit to lead you to Scripture verses that shine the light of God's truth into the deceptions you've believed. The concordance in your Bible comes in handy when you're searching for verses regarding a topic or word you hear from the Lord. Write the Bible verses and references here.

In the power given to you by Jesus Christ, through the shedding of His blood, take authority over the enemy and his attempts to distract and confuse you with his misconceptions. Speak out loud to rebuke the devil and proclaim the truth of God's Word, which you recorded above.

Pray:

Heavenly Father, please forgive me for believing the lies that cause me to worry. I give my worries over to You right now regarding _____. I release _____ to You because You are in control of everything and You work all things together for Your good and mine. Thank You for this opportunity to increase my faith and trust in You, my All-Sufficient Lord. Please take this burden from me and give me Your perfect peace, which exceeds my comprehension and protects my heart and mind. I claim freedom from this anxiety. Father, I know that You will meet all my needs according to Your glorious riches in Christ Jesus. Therefore, I will worry no more and be anxious for nothing, because I trust in You with all my heart. Remove this obstacle and allow me to hear the voice of Your Spirit within me. In Jesus' precious name, I pray. Amen.

Listen:

Lord, what do You want me to know about my worry? (Write down all your thoughts and identify which thoughts may actually be God's voice.)

Chapter 5

Busyness

The Enemy of Freedom

Now the Lord is the Spirit, and where the Spirit of the Lord is, there is freedom. (2 Corinthians 3:17)

When the fire of prayer goes out, the barrenness of busyness takes over.—George Carey

From God's Heart to Yours

Sweet child of Mine, I desire first place in your life. I request your best, your first fruits, not your leftovers. I want the first of your time as well. My plans are to prosper you, to give you hope and a future. I designed you with a specific purpose in mind. How do you know My best for you unless you listen to My voice? How will you receive My wisdom without turning to My Word? How will you know Me without spending time with Me?

*Your best-laid plans may not be **My** best for you. Your life is on GO sixteen hours a day, but how much of that time is dedicated to Me? To My work? Sixty minutes? Twenty? Ten? Any at all? You won't comprehend the great depth of My love for you until you hear My whispers. You can't begin to understand Me when you don't make time for Me. You ask why you do not hear Me. Are you listening? Do you give Me time to speak? I do have something to say.*

Will you meet with Me in the morning?
Will you turn to Me mid-day?
Will you seek My face in the evening?
I do have something to say.

Will you turn off the television?
Will you put your phone away?
Will you shut down the computer?
I do have something to say.

Will you take Me with you golfing?
Will you walk with Me by the bay?
Will you talk to Me in your office?
I do have something to say.

Will you ask Me for My wisdom?
Will you bend your ear My way?
Will you listen with excitement?
I do have something to say.

Will you look for Me when you're lonely?
Will you make time for Me in your day?
Will you call on Me in your trials?
I do have something to say.

Will you recognize My whispers?
Will you listen to Me when you pray?
Will you greet Me with anticipation?
I do have something to say.

Please make time for Me, My friend. I desire to walk through life with you, but I'd prefer to lead. I am with you always. I'll never leave you or forsake you. Please do not forget I am with you at all times, in all places. You are My beloved child. I am pleased by you. I wait with excitement to spend time with you. Please make that happen soon. I am here for you.

BUSYNESS

When we don't have time for God, it's difficult to have a meaningful conversation or relationship with Him. The busyness of life may keep you from hearing God's voice. Satan loves to fill up our lives, even with good, godly acts of service, so that we don't have time to listen to God's voice. The enemy keeps us in chaos and noise so that we cannot hear the still, small voice of Jesus. Are you too busy serving in too many places, so you miss out on what He says to you? Or do you make time regularly to sit alone with the Lord, listening to His Spirit within you? He does have something to say to you.

Remember Mary and Martha? Martha opened her home to Jesus. All her preparations for His visit robbed her of spending time with her Guest of honor, while Mary sat at Jesus' feet and eagerly listened to what He said.

> But Martha was distracted by all the preparations that had to be made. She came to Him and asked, "Lord, don't you care that my sister has left me to do the work by myself? Tell her to help me!"
> "Martha, Martha," the Lord answered, "you are worried and upset about many things, but only one thing is needed. Mary has chosen what is better, and it will not be taken away from her." (Luke 10:40-41)

Are you too busy doing, doing, doing to sit at the feet of Jesus and listen to what He wants to say to you? It pleased Jesus that Mary sat and listened to Him, and He didn't take that time away from her. Everything else could wait.

I must confess, my innate tendency is to behave more like Martha than Mary. Being the die-hard people-pleaser that I am, if Jesus and His disciples came to visit my home, I might be more worried about the hospitality than the relationality. I could see myself scurrying around, cleaning, preparing a meal, and making sure my guests are well taken care of. I would be more inclined to "do" than to "be" still and listen.

Understanding my nature and God-given spiritual gift of help or service, I must force myself to be more social and relational when hosting a gathering. My efforts are usually concentrated on fulfilling the roles of maid, cook, caterer, server, dishwasher, launderer, and concierge, rather than playing the warm, welcoming, congenial hostess role. I'm afraid I would be more concerned about making sure Jesus had a clean, comfortable place to sit, a nice meal to eat, a tasty wine to drink, and crisp, clean sheets to sleep on than on honoring Him with my undivided time, listening to every word that rolled out of His mouth.

Opposites attract, however. My husband is a popular, sanguine Mary. He walks into a crowded room and immediately bursts with positive energy from being in a social atmosphere. He loves communicating with anyone and everyone. He enjoys initiating and carrying on conversations with complete strangers. A social gathering is very exciting and emotionally stimulating for him. He talks and listens to each guest who enters our home, making them feel special and welcome. My husband would shake Jesus's hand and cheerfully sit at His feet, listening to every word He spoke. Whose behavior do you think Jesus would most appreciate? Are you a Martha or a Mary?

When Martha told Jesus to reprimand Mary for not helping her with the preparations, Jesus very clearly set Martha straight on her priorities. We have to find a balance between serving and spending time alone with Christ, listening to His voice. Is Jesus pleased with the amount of individual attention you give Him? Are you making your time with Him a priority over your other activities? Your calendar might be due for an overhaul. Free up some time daily to be with God. Cross off some of the less important activities. Write in ink, not pencil, to schedule your "God" time. Don't let another activity "bump" your time with God or take priority over your relationship with Jesus, the Lord of your life. Perhaps you have fallen prey to some of these misconceptions:

[LIE] **#1: I don't have time to wait for God to speak to me.**

I've been sitting here quietly for twenty minutes waiting for God to speak to me, and I don't hear anything. I don't have time to sit here doing nothing when I have so many things to do today. Do those thoughts hit home for you? Maybe you are already in the practice of faithfully listening for God to speak, but you still don't hear His voice? Well, don't give up yet!

After the first time I heard God speak, I eagerly desired to hear His voice again. Morning after morning I sat quietly at the feet of Jesus waiting to hear something, anything that resembled His still, small voice in my head. For weeks, I heard nothing. I spent the first thirty minutes or so of each morning talking to God and anxiously awaiting an answer from Him.

My husband and I often quote the person who said, "Busy people get things done." I eagerly woke up early and stayed up late— all the hours in between were filled with activities, events, and projects. Sitting quietly, waiting on God to speak, proved extremely difficult and unnatural for me, leaving wide open spaces in my head for me to think of all the other things I could be doing.

It wasn't until I started writing ALL my thoughts in a journal that I realized God did speak to me. Most likely, He had been speaking to me all those days, weeks, months, even years, and I just didn't grasp it. I didn't recognize His voice because I hadn't communicated with Him on a regular basis. I had spoken to Him, but I'd never left room in the conversation for Him to answer me!

TRUTH #1: There is a time for everything.

Most people regularly use the excuse, "I don't have time." Might I point out there is a time for everything? Ecclesiastes 3:1 says, "There is a time for everything, and a season for every activity under heaven." Verse 7 goes on to say, "a time to be silent and a time to speak."

Many times I say, "I don't have time," when what I mean is, "I'm not going to make the time." Any of us can make time for anything. All of us can make time for God. It may mean losing some sleep and setting my alarm to wake me an hour earlier than normal. I may need to give up my free time while the children are napping to spend an hour with Him. Or I may have to trade watching television at night for spending time with Jesus. Whatever takes up too much of my time needs to be scaled back in order to devote the necessary time to God. I may need to read God's Word rather than the latest romance novel or clothing catalog. What daily activity in your life could be rearranged or re-evaluated to allow time to meet with God?

The Truth in God's Word:

There is a time for everything, and a season for every activity under heaven...a time to be silent and a time to speak. (Ecclesiastes 3:1 and 7).

#2: All these other activities I do are more urgent than spending time with God.

This barrier of busyness generally pairs itself with the roadblock of self-righteousness. By the time I reached my mid-thirties, my life calendar resembled attending a popular theme park, and running from one event to the next left no time to spend in relationship with God. In essence, my life screamed: *I don't need You, God, I can do this on my own. I don't have time for You.*

I thought I had a great thing going. I proudly thought of myself as Wonder Woman. I ran on little sleep and had no time to breathe in between the events of the day. I worked full-time, then delivered my children to sporting events and other activities. I led school committees and church ministries. My husband worked hard and played hard, leaving me the responsibilities of a single parent.

Somehow I managed everything and held it all together for years...until the depression struck like lightning, and my power went out.

Life as I knew it came to a screeching halt. My once strong constitution shattered into hundreds of pieces held together by only my skin. Clinical depression disabled me physically, emotionally, and spiritually. I barely managed myself, let alone my home, my children, my job, and all the other capacities I served in. My life quickly spiraled downward until I dwelled in a dark, inescapable pit. But guess what? That's right. It gave me time for God.

God allowed me to hit bottom to get my attention. I couldn't get myself out of this one. My prideful independence crashed me into the wall of self-destruction. Depression not only incapacitated me, but it also humbled me. I had no control over anything in my life, and I had to publicly admit to it.

The price that Jesus paid to save me is unfathomable. You'd think I could respect Him enough to spend a little time each day with Him to show Him my gratitude. However, the misleading whispers in my head told me I didn't need God daily; I managed my life pretty well on my own. Have you ever experienced this attitude?

I believed the lie: *I control my life, and I can handle it all by myself without giving God any of my time. I don't need to lean on Him for anything.* Of course, I didn't realize I had fallen for this devilish deceit. I simply tried to get through each day on my own, doing it my way. I never said I did it easily and successfully. Life is hard, but life without God is harder!

TRUTH #2: Spending time with God is our #1 priority.

God created us and loves us so much, He desires to have a personal, intimate relationship with each one of us. He wants to meet with us daily to shower us with His love, encouragement, kindness, wisdom, guidance, and everything else He has to offer. He desires that we focus our attention on Him first. God wants us to seek Him and to love Him with everything we have: all our heart, soul, mind, and strength. He wants us to call on Him before we put our feet on the floor every morning, speak with Him throughout our day, think of Him at all times in all places, and seek Him in conversational prayer before we close our eyes to sleep each night.

He is Immanuel, God with us 24/7, through the presence of His Holy Spirit, Who indwells every Christ follower. God desires intimate two-way conversation with each of us all day long. He has the answer to every question, the provision for every need, the fulfillment for every longing, the food for the hungry soul, the living water for the thirsty spirit, the strength for every weakness, the protection for every battle, the encouragement for every insecurity, the wisdom for every decision, and the help for every challenge. He exchanges His joy for our sorrow, carries our burdens, leads us through our challenges, and uses our difficulties for His good and ours.

He is our Rock and Redeemer, Savior and Lord, Comforter and Counselor. He is the one true God, Creator of all things. He is the sovereign God of the universe, in control of all things. He is the invincible, omniscient, omnipotent, omnipresent God. And yet He desires intimacy with each of His children—with you and with me. He has a divine plan and a purpose for every person He created. He knows us better than we know ourselves. And He wants to speak with us and relate with us personally every day, all day.

God is so great, why wouldn't we want to speak with Him every day? He is with us at all times, so all we need to do is direct our thoughts inward and be conscious of His Spirit inside us. We can tune in to God's voice within us all day as He speaks to us and guides us. Just as we need to plug in our cell phones and electronic devices to recharge them, our souls need to plug in to God's Holy Spirit, our energy source within, to recharge our spiritual batteries and stay grounded in His will.

Jesus exemplified putting God first when He made time to be alone with His heavenly Father, away from the crowds and noise. He often went to a garden or an out-of-the-way place, where He would spend time praying and receiving direction from God and refreshment from the Spirit.

If your spouse asked you to make him or her your first priority, what would that look like to you? For me it means I would put him before everything else I do. I'd need to manage my time so that my husband received the biggest chunk of it. I'd submit myself to my husband and communicate with him about everything. I'd let him in on my life and accept his wisdom and instruction. I would honor and obey him. I would place my trust in him. Doesn't Jesus, our Bridegroom, deserve this kind of undivided attention and devotion from us for at least the first few minutes of each day He gives us the breath of life? Even more, He never forgets us, and neither should we forget Him as we walk through each day.

One way to love God with all our heart, soul, mind, and strength is to recognize and honor His presence in our lives. When we listen to the voice of His Spirit, trust God, and obey Him, He feels loved.

The Truth in God's Word:

"You shall have no other gods before Me." (Deuteronomy 5:7)

"Love the Lord your God with all your heart and with all your soul and with all your strength. These commandments that I give you today are to be upon your hearts. Impress them on your children. Talk about them when you sit at home and when you walk along the road, when you lie down and when you get up. Tie them as symbols on your hands and bind them on your foreheads. Write them on the doorframes of your houses and on your gates." (Deuteronomy 6:5-9)

Hearing that Jesus had silenced the Sadducees, the Pharisees got together. One of them, an expert in the law, tested Him with this question: "Teacher, which is the greatest commandment in the Law?" Jesus replied: "'Love the Lord your God with all your heart and with all your soul and with all your mind.' This is the first and greatest commandment." (Matthew 22:34-38)

"But seek *first* His kingdom and His righteousness, and all these things will be given to you as well." (Matthew 6:33; emphasis mine)

And they did not do as we expected, but *they gave themselves first to the Lord* and then to us in keeping with God's will. (2 Corinthians 8:5; emphasis mine)

LIE #3: Investing time in godly activities equals having a relationship with Jesus.

When I accepted Jesus Christ as my Savior, He began transforming my life. I tried to eliminate activities and behaviors that were unbecoming to a Christ follower and ramped up my Christian practices. I worshipped in church twice on Sunday. I traded my pop, rock, and country music for contemporary Christian music. I changed the country station in my car to Christian radio. I completed small group Bible studies. I read daily devotionals and Christian self-help books. I prayed and served in church ministries. I tried not to sin too much, and when I did, I asked for forgiveness. All this meant that I enjoyed a relationship with Jesus, right? Not necessarily. Did I really enjoy "relationship" with Jesus, or did I simply practice religion?

I hope you are not convinced, as I was, that doing these things daily in honor of Jesus equals having a relationship with Him. While all these activities might be an important part of the Christian life, they do not match spiritual intimacy with the Lord through two-way communication.

TRUTH #3: A relationship with Jesus is more than practicing good, religious activities daily.

A man and woman can practice great marriage enrichment activities daily, but it doesn't guarantee they'll enjoy an emotionally or physically intimate relationship. A husband and wife may give nice gifts to each other, read books on building a strong marriage, enjoy a weekly date night, serve one another daily, and sleep in the same bed every night; however, those activities, either alone or in total, do not promise an emotionally or physically intimate relationship if the spouses do not talk to each other and listen to one another daily. Good communication—spending time in healthy two-way conversation—is the key to emotional and spiritual intimacy between a bride and groom, as well as between the bride of Christ and her Bridegroom—you and Jesus.

Attaining emotional and physical intimacy in any relationship rests in *time dedicated to continuous, good, verbal two-way communication*. A spiritually intimate relationship with God requires the same.

Twenty years into being a Christ follower, I didn't really understand that I practiced "religion" rather than "relationship with Jesus." Accepting Jesus Christ as your Savior is the *beginning* of your relationship with Him. The moment you confess "with your mouth, 'Jesus is Lord,' and believe in your heart that God raised Him from the dead, you will be saved" (see Romans 10:9-10). God sends His Holy Spirit to live in your heart. That should make it easy to enjoy a relationship with Jesus, right? His Spirit dwells within each believer. So why did I feel so empty and alone? All those Christian activities did not fill the void in my heart, and neither did God's Spirit—until I quit talking to God and started listening to Him.

I already mentioned that God used my periods of clinical depression to help me understand my complete dependence on Him and to nurture me into a more intimate relationship with Him. When I dwelled at the bottom of the pit, UP was the only direction to travel. Depression rocked me and my Wonder Woman inner strength crumbled. In my broken state, I no longer wanted to "practice" religion. In fact, I felt no desire, ambition, or fortitude to pray or read God's Word at all during that dark time. In tears, all I could do was utter a few words to Jesus, hoping He knew what I needed.

With sketchy faith, groping for a reason to go on, I approached God one night, asking Him to tell me who I am to Him. I wasn't leaving without an answer. At that moment, it seemed I put myself all in. I sought God with all my heart, soul, mind, and strength, which didn't amount to much at that time, but it was all I had to give Him.

Jesus *did* know exactly what I needed. He spoke to me. I heard His voice, undeniably, that first time. It required closing my mouth and opening my ears, waiting in anticipation. That evening, I discovered the truth. God is *alive* and He cares about me. That was all I needed to go on. That was the first day of the rest of my life.

As I learned to listen for God over the following months, I began daily to submit myself to the Lordship of Jesus Christ and *spend time with Him in healthy, two-way communication*. The relationship developed and matured as I met with Jesus every day, talking to Him, and leaving room in the conversation for Him to speak to me. I listened and obeyed as He directed me on the paths He had laid out for me. For the first time, I read the Bible enthusiastically, eager to learn everything I could about God, Jesus, and the Holy Spirit. He drew me into His Word and made Scripture come alive for me, time after time. He revealed more of Himself and more of who I am in Christ.

Finally, I understood what other people meant when they talked about a *relationship* with Jesus Christ. I now have one, and it is truly the best thing Jesus has done for me, second only to hanging on the cross for my sin. You may be praying or talking to God, but are you listening to Him? Two-way conversation with God will bring dry bones to life and make dead hearts come alive. God desires intimacy with all of His children. Will you make time for Him?

The Truth in God's Word:

As a bridegroom rejoices over his bride, so will your God rejoice over you. (Isaiah 62:5)

"But the Counselor, the Holy Spirit, Whom the Father will send in My name, will teach you all things and will remind you of everything I have said to you." (John 14:26)

"You are already clean because of the word I have spoken to you. Remain in Me, and I will remain in you. No branch can bear fruit by itself; it must remain in the vine. Neither can you bear fruit unless you remain in Me. I am the vine; you are the branches. If a man remains in Me and I in him, he will bear much fruit; apart from Me you can do nothing. If anyone does not remain in Me, he is like a branch that is thrown away and withers; such branches are picked up, thrown into the fire and burned. If you remain in Me and My words remain in you, ask whatever you wish, and it will be given you. This is to My Father's glory, that you bear much fruit, showing yourselves to be My disciples. As the Father has loved Me, so have I loved you. Now remain in My love. If you obey My commands, you will remain in My love, just as I have obeyed My Father's commands and remain in His love." (John 15:3-10)

Listen to God's heart about busyness in His Word and His communications to me in the following *Manna for Today* excerpts.

✝

Therefore, since we are surrounded by such a great cloud of witnesses, let us throw off everything that hinders and the sin that so easily entangles, and let us run with perseverance the race marked out for us. Let us fix our eyes on Jesus, the author and perfecter of our faith, who for the joy set before Him endured the cross, scorning its shame, and sat down at the right hand of the throne of God. Consider Him who endured such opposition from sinful men, so that you will not grow weary and lose heart (Hebrews 12:1-3).

Persevere[16]

My love, do not grow weary and lose heart. Your opponent loves to busy up your life so that you do not have time or energy for Me. Do not take on too many "good" things, but seek Me to know My "best" for you. The enemy's mission is to hinder you from Me. He enjoys presenting you with great opportunities that will exhaust your time. He loves to tie you up in bondage to sin, and then accuse you and shame you into his submission. Be alert! I have already won this battle. You are victorious in Jesus Christ.

My Son endured death on a cross to pay for your sin and bail you out of your destination to eternal damnation. Do not lose sight of what Jesus has already done for you. Press on toward the goal. I have marked out a race for you. Your finish line is marked by the gates of heaven. Run with perseverance. Do not let the enemy cut in on you, and distract you from achieving your goal of eternity with Me. I hold the stopwatch. I govern this race.

Fix your eyes on Me alone. Run toward Me, and do not look back. Do not step to the left or to the right. Placing your foot on another path that I have not cleared for you may cause you to stumble and fall. Be steadfast in your commitment to Me. Your dedication will reward you one hundred-fold. My blessings are abundant for the unwavering, faithful one. Celebrate your

---

[16] Sindy Nagel, "Persevere" in *Manna for Today: Bread from Heaven for Each Day* (Bloomington, IN: WestBow Press 2012), 150.

victory in Me! The race has been won. You will spend eternity with Me in the place I have prepared for you. Persevere and stay on track. Do not grow weary and lose heart. Continue in the right direction, and your inheritance from the Lord will be your reward.

Now may the Lord of peace Himself give you peace at all times and in every way. The Lord be with all of you (2 Thessalonians 3:16).

Prince of Peace[17]

Peace I give you, for I am the Prince of Peace. I am always with you. I am the peace you need. Your world is so busy. Your time is all tied up. You have so little time for Me, but when you remain in Me, I will give you peace. Spend time with Me away from the noise and activity. I will give you peace during your most stressful times. My peace is accompanied by confidence and joy— the confidence of knowing that I am in control, and the joy of knowing that I love you and take care of you.

When your day is planned from start to finish with no room for Me, it may feel to you as if I am not with you, but I am. I walk with you every step of the way. I wait patiently for you to seek Me. When you rush ahead in the plans you have made for yourself, sometimes you feel unappreciated and empty by the end of the day. I would fill you up with My Spirit, if only you would ask. When you know Me, there is no reason to feel empty. I am here. I love you. I appreciate you. I want to spend time with you. I want to replace your stress with a calm spirit. I want to fill you with My love. I want to cover you with My joy and peace.

Be confident in knowing that I am in control. Leave room in your day for Me. Allow Me to map out your time. Your prosperity is very important to Me. You can live a good life without Me, but will it be My best for you? My ways are higher than your ways. I know what is best for you. Will you trust

---

[17] Sindy Nagel, "Prince of Peace" in *Manna for Today: Bread from Heaven for Each Day* (Bloomington, IN: WestBow Press 2012), 133.

Me to lead you in that direction, even when it may not be consistent with your plans? Cast all your anxieties on Me. I will give you rest. Rest in my arms, and allow Me to carry you down this road you are on. I will build you up, and when I set you down, you will run in the confidence of My commands. I know the plans I have for you. My peace is inlaid in the steps I have marked out for you. Go in the peace I designed for you.

Two are better than one, because they have a good return for their work: If one falls down, his friend can help him up. But pity the man who falls and has no one to help him up! (Ecclesiastes 4:9-10)

Two are Better than One[18]

My child, I am so happy that you come to me when you feel overwhelmed by life. You do not have the energy or the frame of mind you need to accomplish your tasks today? Your head is clouded, and you are not able to focus on your work? Do not feel overcome with shame and sadness at your present state. Shame is from the evil one. When you are not able to begin or accomplish what you have set out to do, it may be because you attempt it alone.

When you do not spend time with Me first, you start off on the wrong foot, but now, you have come to the right place. I am your source of life. You will do all things by My strength. On your own, you may not accomplish as much, but with Me, together we will do great things. Two are better than one. You will have a better return for your work when you are yoked with Me. If you fall down, I am there to pick you up. Join yourself with Me.

My beloved one, you are good because you are Mine. My "to-do" list for you will not overwhelm you. You have only one thing to do today—spend time with Me. Seek Me, tell Me, listen to Me, follow Me, and rest in Me. That is all I have for you to accomplish today. The remainder of the day will take care

---

[18] Sindy Nagel, "Two are Better than One" in *Manna for Today: Bread from Heaven for Each Day* (Bloomington, IN: WestBow Press 2012), 151.

of itself. There is a time to work and a time to have fun. There is a time to plant and a time to reap. There is a time to be busy and a time to be still. There is a time for everything under heaven.

Today, you will be still and rest in Me. My yoke is easy and My burden is light. Partner with Me today. Two are better than one. We will accomplish much more together than you could ever accomplish on your own. Step forward first with your right foot as I step forward with Mine; your left foot will follow. My steps are not too big for you. Put one foot in front of the other in the path I map out for you. As we walk it together, everything else will fall into order. Should you stumble, you will not fall, for I am here to help you. I give you My hand.

Find satisfaction in your work today. Take delight in what you set your hands to do. No task is too large; no task is too meaningless, but all work done with Me by your side is toil worth the effort. To those who please Me, I give wisdom, knowledge, and happiness. You are pleasing to Me because you have taken time for Me today. Be at ease with your life, and leave your worries to Me. You are not alone; you are with Me, and two are better than one.

✝

Self-Reflection:

1. Describe a time when you gave in to your industrious Martha role, rather than sitting at Jesus' feet, like Mary.

2. What do you think you missed out on by being too busy to listen to Jesus?

3. What do you desire to hear Jesus say to you?

4. Sit alone with Jesus right now. Close your eyes and focus on making Him your first priority. Eliminate all distractions and be still before the Lord. Tell God what you love about Him.

5. Keeping your eyes closed, ask Him to rejoice over you right now. Do you see Him in your mind? What is He doing? What is He saying? Journal your thoughts.

6. Ask the Lord whatever pops into your mind. What is His response to you?

7. How will you cause yourself to be conscious of God's presence throughout your day? How will you remember to listen for His voice all day long? Write some ideas here:

Removing the Barrier of Busyness

Ask God to expose the lies and help you identify any false beliefs that cause a barrier of busyness between you and God. Record them here.

Request that God bring memories to your mind of His presence in your life as it relates to your struggles with busyness. Pay close attention to what He is doing and saying to you in your thoughts. Write it down here.

Allow the Holy Spirit to lead you to Scripture verses that shine the light of God's truth into the deceptions you've believed. The concordance in your Bible comes in handy when you're searching for verses regarding a topic or word you hear from the Lord. Write the Bible verses and references here.

In the power given to you by Jesus Christ, through the shedding of His blood, take authority over the enemy and his attempts to distract and confuse you with his misconceptions. Speak out loud to rebuke the devil and proclaim the truth of God's Word, which you recorded above.

Pray:

Sovereign Lord, You are my one and only God. Forgive me for busying up my own schedule so I don't have time for You. Please help me to throw off all the things that hinder me and entangle me. Let me know which activities to lay down so I have more time to spend with You. I want to run the race You have marked out for me. You know what's best for me. Please prune the activities from my calendar that are not ordained by You. You are my Lord, and I want You to lead me in the plans You've made for me. I want to sit at Your feet and listen to every word that falls from Your mouth. Help me to clear time for You in my busy schedule. I desire to put you above everything else and make You my first priority every day. Let peace and quiet be the new normal for me. Let me be comfortable in the silence, patiently waiting to hear Your voice. I desire an intimate relationship with You. Lord, I want to remember You and feel Your presence all day long. I know You are always with me. Hide me from the enemy and his efforts to tie me up in busyness. I want to seek Your wisdom for each opportunity that presents itself to me. Allow me to know the purpose for which You created me and live into that calling, rather than creating my own agenda. In the name of Jesus, my Lord, I pray. Amen.

Listen:

Lord, what do You want me to know about my busyness? (Write down all your thoughts and identify which thoughts may actually be God's voice.)

Chapter 6

Disobedience
The Enemy of Righteousness

Don't you know that when you offer yourselves to someone to obey him as slaves, you are slaves to the one whom you obey—whether you are slaves to sin, which leads to death, or to obedience, which leads to righteousness? (Romans 6:16)

You see, rebellion, and the disobedience it causes, keeps us from having the power of God that's available to us as Christians.—Joyce Meyer

From God's Heart to Yours

My special angel, you have been adopted by Me. I call you by name. You are Mine. You are in the world but not of it. You once walked in the flesh, but now you walk in the Spirit. Do not stray down the path of darkness when My Spirit is there to illuminate your steps. Live by the Spirit's power, keeping in step with the Spirit, and do not gratify the desires of the sinful nature.

Do not be conformed to the patterns of this world. Your old nature and misdeeds have been put to death. Behold! All things are new. My Spirit continues to transform you into My likeness with ever-increasing glory. Be a reflection of Me, and let the light of My goodness shine forth from your countenance.

Do not stoop to acts of disobedience that dishonor Me. When you love Me, you will obey My commands. I desire spiritual intimacy with you. However, sin puts a large valley between us. Do not resort to acts of lawlessness and distance yourself from Me. Your sins will not go unpunished. Therefore, turn from all unrighteous acts and live in obedience to Me.

My beloved child, you have been chosen by Me; you belong to Me. I have called you out of darkness and into My wonderful light. Walk as a child of the light. Do not veer to the right or to the left. Take the narrow path; the wide one surely leads to destruction. Renew your mind, setting it on what the Spirit desires. The mind controlled by the Spirit is life and peace. You who are led by the Spirit are God's children. The Spirit testifies to the same.

My Spirit helps you in your weakness. He intercedes for you in accordance with My will. The Spirit knows the mind of God and reveals the things of God. Therefore, do not be deaf to the Spirit, to the very words of God. You know My voice. You have the mind of Christ. You need only listen to My Spirit, Who dwells in you, and you will possess all the wisdom and power you need to obey Me. In the righteousness I give you, draw near to Me and I will draw near to you.

DISOBEDIENCE

It's pretty simple—disobedience to God is sin. Clearly, sin separates us from God. He despises sin and doesn't want to be anywhere near it. Isaiah 59:1-2 says, "Surely the arm of the Lord is not too short to save, nor His ear too dull to hear. But your iniquities have separated you from your God; your sins have hidden His face from you, so that He will not hear." This verse confirms that sin and an unrepentant heart can keep God from hearing you. When He hides His face from you, most likely, He will not speak to you either. Does sin, or disobedience, stand in your way of hearing God's voice?

Confession of sin is not only required by God—it is necessary for your own peace of mind. Confessing your sin, turning from it, and attempting to lead a clean life of obedience open the door of communication between you and God. In our humanness, we won't ever be completely free of sin on earth, but we should try to live our lives in a different way than the rest of the world.

Of course, if you've never confessed your sin and accepted Jesus as your Savior and Lord, then you already live apart from God, and the Holy Spirit does not occupy your heart. In that case, you should not expect to hear God's voice within at all. If that's you, please return to the **Good News** section near the beginning of this book to learn more about how to invite Jesus into your heart and begin a new relationship with Him. When you do, God's Holy Spirit, and the ability to hear His voice, are God's amazing gifts to you.

1 John 1:8-10 says, "If we claim to be without sin, we deceive ourselves and the truth is not in us. If we confess our sins, He is faithful and just and will forgive us our sins and purify us from all unrighteousness. If we claim we have not sinned, we make Him out to be a liar and His word has no place in our lives." Sounds like it's not *if* we sin, but *when* we sin, confession is required. Then, God is faithful to forgive us and cleanse us. Our full acceptance of His pardon releases us from all guilt and shame for that offense. God remembers our sins no more, so we can forget them also, and strive to do better next time we are tempted.

Even after accepting Christ as my Savior and being a Christian for many years, it's still nearly impossible to live a sin-free life. That's the goal, but sadly, in my humanness, it's not achievable on this side of the pearly gates. Jesus is the only person who ever accomplished that feat. One role of the Holy Spirit is to empower me to overcome temptation and resist sin. However, if I am not tuned in constantly, listening to God's voice within, or if I am not willing to obey Him, I will fall short of God's glory. Therefore, it's still possible, on any given day, that disobedience, unconfessed sin, rebellion, or repetitive sin could erect a roadblock that impedes my clear communication with God.

After being a Christ follower for nearly thirty-five years, I still mess up daily. How sad! I love Jesus; I am grateful for His amazing, selfless act of hanging on the cross on my behalf; but somehow, I still find myself daily heaping more of my sin on His shoulders. It's not usually intentional. I don't consciously do it on purpose—or do I? Regretfully, if I am truthful, at times I *do* know I'm acting in disobedience to God. How awful is that? I admit, it's pretty terrible. I can relate to Paul's confession in Romans 7:14-25:

> We know that the law is spiritual; but I am unspiritual, sold as a slave to sin. I do not understand what I do. For what I want to do I do not do, but what I hate I do. And if I do what I do not want to do, I agree that the law is good. As it is, it is no longer I myself who do it, but it is sin living in me. I know that nothing good lives in me, that is, in my sinful nature. For I have the desire to do what is good, but I cannot carry it out. For what I do is not the good I want to do; no, the evil I do not want to do—this I keep on doing. Now if I do what I do not want to do, it is no longer I who do it, but it is sin living in me that does it.
> So I find this law at work: When I want to do good, evil is right there with me. For in my inner being I delight in God's law; but I see another law at work in the members of my body, waging war against the law of my mind and making me a prisoner of the law of sin at work within my members. What a wretched man I am! Who will rescue me from this body of death? Thanks be to God—through Jesus Christ our Lord!
> So then, I myself in my mind am a slave to God's law, but in the sinful nature a slave to the law of sin.

No matter how hard we try to defeat sin, at times, it becomes our master. Thankfully, we serve a High Priest who hears our confessions and daily intercedes on our behalf, restoring our relationships with God the Father. We worship an awesome God who sent His Son to be a sin offering in place of us, and then, He also sent us the gift of the indwelling Holy Spirit to empower us to live our lives according to the Spirit rather than the sinful nature. In Romans 8:5-12, Paul offers a better outlook to us, who belong to Christ:

> Those who live according to the sinful nature have their minds set on what that nature desires; but those who live in accordance with the Spirit have their minds set on what the Spirit desires. The mind of sinful man is death, but the mind controlled by the Spirit is life and peace, the sinful mind is hostile to God. It does not submit to God's law, nor can it do so. Those controlled by the sinful nature cannot please God.
> You, however, are controlled not by the sinful nature but by the Spirit, if the Spirit of God lives in you. And if anyone does not have the Spirit of Christ, he does not belong to Christ. But if Christ is in you, your body is dead because of sin, yet your spirit is alive because of righteousness. And if the Spirit of Him Who raised Jesus from the dead is living in you, He Who raised Christ from the dead will also give life to your mortal bodies through His Spirit, Who lives in you.

Satan has only as much power as we give him. How powerless have you become? Whatever your weakness, it's time to take back control! All of it! We've been given Jesus' authority over all sin. We have the same power that raised Jesus from the dead, and He lives inside us. Instead of relinquishing our power to the adversary, we must draw on the strength of the Holy Spirit within us to resist temptation and our tendency to believe the lies Satan introduces in our thoughts. We have the ability stand firm in our faith and resist all temptation because the Lord does not allow us to be tempted beyond what we can handle. "No temptation has seized you except what is common to man. And God is faithful; He will not let you be tempted beyond what you can bear. But when you are tempted, He will also provide a way out so that you can stand up under it." (1 Corinthians 10:13)

Our brothers and sisters in Christ, who live in all parts of the world, suffer similar trials.

> Be self-controlled and alert. Your enemy the devil prowls around like a roaring lion looking for someone to devour. Resist him, standing firm in the faith, because you know that your brothers throughout the world are undergoing the same kind of sufferings.
> And the God of all grace, who called you to His eternal glory in Christ, after you have suffered a little while, will Himself restore you and make you strong, firm and steadfast. To Him be the power for ever and ever. Amen. (1 Peter 5:8-11)

Be vigilant about guarding your heart and your mind. Do not allow the deceiver to carry out his battle plans on your watch. Take your thoughts captive and make them obedient to Jesus Christ. Dr.

Charles F. Stanley[19] offers a great explanation of Satan's deception in our minds:

> **Satan deceives believers.** His battlefield is our minds, and his plan is to lead us astray from devotion to Christ (2 Cor.11:3). He brings up old memories of hurts and mistreatment so we will dwell on them and experience the suffering again. The only way to protect ourselves from his deception is to fill our minds with God's Word.

In 2 Corinthians 11:3, Paul says, "But I am afraid that just as Eve was deceived by the serpent's cunning, your minds may somehow be led astray from your sincere and pure devotion to Christ." How do we keep from being led astray? By filling our minds with God's Word. We must follow Paul's charge to us in 2 Corinthians 10:3-5:

> For though we live in the world, we do not wage war as the world does. The weapons we fight with are not the weapons of the world. On the contrary, they have divine power to demolish strongholds. We demolish arguments and every pretension that sets itself up against the knowledge of God, and we take captive every thought to make it obedient to Christ.

---

[19] Dr. Charles F. Stanley, *Taking Control of Your Thoughts* (InTouch Ministries, intouch.org, Sermon Notes SN140817, 2015).

The weapons we fight with are the sword of the Spirit, which is the Word of God, and the power of God's Spirit within us. Bathe yourself daily in Scripture, and verbally clothe yourself every day in the Armor of God from Ephesians 6:10-18, which says:

> Finally, be strong in the Lord and in His mighty power. Put on the full armor of God so that you can take your stand against the devil's schemes. For our struggle is not against flesh and blood, but against the rulers, against the authorities, against the powers of this dark world and against the spiritual forces of evil in the heavenly realms. Therefore put on the full armor of God, so that when the day of evil comes, you may be able to stand your ground, and after you have done everything, to stand. Stand firm then, with the belt of truth buckled around your waist, with the breastplate of righteousness in place, and with your feet fitted with the readiness that comes from the gospel of peace. In addition to all this, take up the shield of faith, with which you can extinguish all the flaming arrows of the evil one. Take the helmet of salvation and the sword of the Spirit, which is the Word of God. And pray in the Spirit on all occasions with all kinds of prayers and requests. With this in mind, be alert and always keep on praying for all the saints.

When I stood on the sidelines of life and did not participate in the big game, the devil did not need to concentrate his focus on me. The moment I invited Jesus into my heart and sought a more intimate relationship with Him, I enlisted in the battle of good vs. evil. Choosing God's side, I put a large target on my back for the dragon, Satan, to take his aim. Satan sat up, took notice, and stepped-up his plan of action to derail me.

The final book of the Bible describes how Satan feels about God's children. Revelation 12:17 says, "Then the dragon was enraged at the woman and went off to make war against the rest of her offspring—those who obey God's commandments and hold to the testimony of Jesus." These mind battles will not be ending any time soon. Probably, the dragon will not back down and run away with his tail between his legs in our lifetime. He will continue to sway us toward disobedience. But Jesus triumphantly conquered this battle for us already. We can claim our victory over sin in the name and blood of Jesus Christ.

Are you ready to stand firm in your faith and embark on a barrier-free journey of intimacy with Jesus? If your desire is to do so, but you feel unprepared, I suggest you beef up your plan of counterattack against temptation and sin by practicing these steps **daily**:

- ❖ Confess your sin.

- ❖ Turn from your disobedient ways.

- ❖ Immerse yourself in the Word of God. Meditate on it day and night.

- ❖ Dress yourself in the full armor of God.

- ❖ Be ready to draw the sword of the Spirit by being prepared with Scripture to battle temptation and lies.

- ❖ Know your weak spots and vulnerabilities.
- ❖ Take control of all your thoughts and make them obedient to Christ.
- ❖ Remove any other roadblocks between you and God.
- ❖ Listen to the still, small voice of the Holy Spirit all day long.
- ❖ Obey the voice of God in your thoughts.

Has the devil ever captivated your thoughts with the following deceptions? If not the lies listed below, then identify any other lies regarding sin that you have believed and disprove them with the truth from Scripture.

LIE

#1: Your sins are too big for God to forgive.

Satan wanted me to believe my sins outweighed God's grace; I was not fully forgiven. I was convinced forgiveness for the sins I had committed required more than confessing them and accepting Christ's death on the cross as payment in full. When I say that out loud, it sounds absolutely ridiculous. To discount and minimize the atoning work of Christ and even consider it wasn't enough to redeem me from my sin is rather disconcerting, but that's how the deceiver works. God's plan of salvation is perfect. God had forgiven me;

however, I had not fully accepted His grace and forgiveness. When we confess our sin, God is faithful and just and will forgive us our sin—all of it, no matter how big or small the offense (see 1 John 1:9). After I spent time meditating on God's Word and plan of salvation, the Holy Spirit enlightened my heart and mind to the truth. I had confessed my sin, accepted Christ as my Savior, and invited Him into my heart to be my Lord. At that moment, He forgave and forgot every sin I had committed. He washed me whiter than snow and offered me a fresh start. I had received a second chance to turn away from my sin and practice living in obedience to God.

The Apostle Paul proclaimed himself to be the worst sinner of all, yet the grace and mercy of Jesus Christ were abundant enough to save him. No sin is too big for God to forgive. Read the confession of Paul from 1 Timothy 1:12-17:

> I thank Christ Jesus our Lord, who has given me strength, that He considered me faithful, appointing me to His service. Even though I was once a blasphemer and a persecutor and a violent man, I was shown mercy because I acted in ignorance and unbelief. The grace of our Lord was poured out on me abundantly, along with the faith and love that are in Christ Jesus.
> Here is a trustworthy saying that deserves full acceptance: Christ Jesus came into the world to save sinners—of whom I am the worst. But for that very reason I was shown mercy so that in me, the worst of sinners, Christ Jesus might display His unlimited patience as an example for those who would believe on Him and receive eternal life. Now to the King

eternal, immortal, invisible, the only God, be honor and glory for ever and ever. Amen.

If God can forgive Paul—who intentionally, blatantly, publicly disrespected and defiled the name of Jesus while mistreating, abusing, tormenting, and torturing Christ followers— God's grace is sufficient for you and me. We simply need to spend time with Him and read Scripture about His character to grasp His limitless kindness and blessing to all those who have repented.

TRUTH #1: When you confess your sin, God is faithful and just and will forgive it (see 1 John 1:9).

Have you ever felt that your sins are unforgivable? Let me assure you, they are not. As I mentioned above, at times I wondered if God could really forgive my sins, or were they too large? Why did I feel I needed to keep asking God's forgiveness for the same old sins even though I was a new creation in Christ, the old ways were gone, and I hadn't returned to them? Was my sin too big for God to forgive, or was God's forgiveness too big for me to grasp?

No sin is too big for God to forgive. In 1 Corinthians 6:9-11, Paul assures the new Christ followers who previously were sexually immoral, idolaters, adulterers, male prostitutes, homosexuals, thieves, greedy, drunkards, slanderers, and swindlers, "But you were washed, you were sanctified, you were justified in the name of the Lord Jesus Christ and by the Spirit of our God." The sins of the Corinthians may seem bigger than some of your sins. Or possibly you feel your sin is greater than those mentioned here. However, all sin equals disobedience to God, and no sin is too big for God to forgive.

When you accepted that Jesus Christ died for your sins, and you invited Him into your heart to be your Savior and the Lord of your life, He wiped your sin debt clean. By His death on the cross, He paid the penalty for all your sins—past, present, and future. By His resurrection, He made it possible for you to know and experience a living God who dwells in you. Jesus cleansed you of all unrighteousness, and the Holy Spirit continues to sanctify you through and through (see 1 Thessalonians 5:23-24).

It turns out, my sins were not too great for Jesus to forgive, but His forgiveness was too big for me to comprehend. Once I dug deeper into God's Word and more fully understood His plan of salvation, I could more fully appreciate His amazing grace and *accept* His forgiveness. Then I could let go of the guilt and shame I tightly held and claim the freedom that His forgiveness offered me. I no longer dwelled in the prison of my past sin, but I lived the life of peace that God intended for me, and I experienced a new confidence in Christ that I didn't own before.

Have you asked Jesus to forgive you? He has. Have you fully accepted His forgiveness? If not, dive into Scripture to more completely understand and appreciate His plan of salvation and His promises. You are a child of God. You are forgiven. You have been washed, sanctified, and justified in the name of the Lord Jesus Christ and by the Spirit of God. Enjoy the peace and freedom that a Spirit-filled life offers you.

The Truth in God's Word:

If we claim to be without sin, we deceive ourselves and the truth is not in us. If we confess our sins, He is faithful and just and will forgive us our sins and purify us from all unrighteousness. If we claim we have not sinned, we make Him out to be a liar and His word has no place in our lives. (1 John 1:8-10)

Do you not know that the wicked will not inherit the kingdom of God? Do not be deceived: Neither the sexually immoral nor idolaters nor adulterers nor male prostitutes nor homosexual offenders nor thieves nor the greedy nor drunkards nor slanderers nor swindlers will inherit the kingdom of God. And that is what some of you were. But you were washed, you were sanctified, you were justified in the name of the Lord Jesus Christ and by the Spirit of our God. (1 Corinthians 6:9-11)

My dear children, I write this to you so that you will not sin. But if anybody does sin, we have one who speaks to the Father in our defense—Jesus Christ, the Righteous One. He is the atoning sacrifice for our sins, and not only for ours but also for the sins of the whole world. (1 John 2:1-2)

Put to death, therefore, whatever belongs to your earthly nature: sexual immorality, impurity, lust, evil desires and greed, which is idolatry. Because of these, the wrath of God is coming. You used to walk in these ways, in the life you once lived. But now you must rid yourselves of all such things as these: anger, rage, malice, slander, and filthy language from your lips. Do not lie to each other, since you have taken off your old self with its practices and have put on the new self, which is being renewed in knowledge in the image of its Creator. (Colossians 3:5-10)

May God Himself, the God of peace, sanctify you through and through. May your whole spirit, soul and body be kept blameless at the coming of our Lord Jesus Christ. The One who calls you is faithful and He will do it. (1 Thessalonians 5:23-24)

[LIE] #2: You need to keep asking for forgiveness for the same sin.

If you continue to live in sin, repeatedly committing the same sin over and over again, then you need to repeatedly ask the Lord's forgiveness for that sin. However, true repentance means turning away from your sin and walking in relationship with and obedience to Jesus Christ. God sent His Holy Spirit to strengthen us for this difficult task. He knows we are weak in the flesh, so His Spirit gives us the power to live in obedience to Christ.

Forgiveness is a gift. God, the Giver, graciously provided a way for our righteousness to be restored by the death of His own Son, Jesus, as full payment for all our sins. We can choose to reject that free gift or accept it. When we reject it, we remain in bondage. We give power over to the prince of darkness, allowing him to continually remind us of our iniquities. But Jesus came to deliver us from evil, set us free from the bondage of sin, and restore abundant life to us through a renewed, right relationship with God the Father. God loves us so much that He desires to connect with us daily through two-way communication. Cut the ties that bind you to your past, and live in the freedom a life in Christ affords you today.

Consider the words of Dr. Charles F. Stanley[20]:

> Are there sins from your past that continue to hang over you like a cloud? Do you doubt that God hears you because of sinful choices you've made? Do you feel that your potential for the kingdom of God has been destroyed?
>
> If you answered yes to any of these questions, you have not yet come to grips with God's solution to your sin. You are still holding on to a way of thinking that can keep you in bondage for the rest of your days on earth. You have set yourself up for a defeated life in which you will never reach your potential in the kingdom of God.
>
> God wants you to be free. And because He does, He sacrificed what was dearest to Him...When you can see yourself as a forgiven child, you will be able to enjoy fellowship with the Father, which was made

---

[20] Dr. Charles F. Stanley, *Freely Forgiven* (www.intouch.org/read/freely-forgiven, 2015) Adapted from Charles F. Stanley, *The Gift of Forgiveness* (Nashville, TN: Thomas Nelson Inc. 1991).

possible by the death of His Son. Then you can begin to fulfill His marvelous calling on your life.

TRUTH #2: The blood of Christ erases our sins and God forgets them, so we should forget them, too.

Hebrews 8-10 offers a great explanation of the New Covenant between God and His people. For our purposes, below are excerpts from these chapters and other passages that encapsulate the old law vs. the new covenant. Whereas the old law required that nearly everything be cleansed with the blood of animals and stated that without the shedding of blood there was no forgiveness (see Hebrews 9:22), the new covenant is that the blood of Christ was shed once for all the sins of all people.

> When everything had been arranged like this, the priests entered regularly into the outer room [of the tabernacle, called the Holy Place] to carry on their ministry. But only the high priest entered the inner room, [the Most Holy Place], and that only once a year, and never without blood, which he offered for himself and for the sins the people had committed in ignorance. The Holy Spirit was showing by this that the way into the Most Holy Place had not yet been disclosed as long as the first tabernacle was still standing. This is an illustration for the present time, indicating that the gifts and sacrifices being offered were not able to clear the conscience of the worshiper. They are only a matter of food and drink

and various ceremonial washings—external regulations applying until the time of the new order.

When Christ came as High Priest of the good things that are already here, He went through the greater and more perfect tabernacle that is not man-made, that is to say, not a part of this creation. He did not enter by means of the blood of goats and calves; but *He entered the Most Holy Place once for all by His own blood*, having obtained eternal redemption. The blood of goats and bulls and the ashes of a heifer sprinkled on those who are ceremonially unclean sanctify them so that they are outwardly clean. *How much more, then, will the blood of Christ, Who through the eternal Spirit offered Himself unblemished to God, cleanse our consciences from acts that lead to death, so that we may serve the living God!* For this reason, Christ is the mediator of a new covenant, that those who are called may receive the promised eternal inheritance—now that He has died as a ransom to set them free from the sins committed under the first covenant. (Hebrews 9:6-15; emphasis mine)

But because Jesus lives forever, He has a permanent priesthood. Therefore He is able to save *completely* those who come to God through Him, because He always lives to intercede for them. Such a high priest meets our need—One Who is holy, blameless, pure, set apart from sinners, exalted above the heavens. Unlike the other high priests, *He does not need to offer sacrifices day after day*, first for His own sins, and then for the sins of the people. *He sacrificed for their sins once for all when He offered Himself.* For the law appoints as high priests men who are weak; but the oath, which came after the law, appointed the Son, Who has been made perfect forever. (Hebrews 7:24-28; emphasis mine)

> Grace and peace to you from Him Who is, and Who was, and Who is to come, and from the seven spirits before His throne, and from Jesus Christ, Who is the faithful witness, the firstborn from the dead, and the ruler of the kings of the earth.
> To Him Who loves us and has *freed us from our sins by His blood*, and has made us to be a kingdom and priests to serve His God and Father—to Him be glory and power for ever and ever! Amen. (Revelation 1:4-6; emphasis mine)

These passages assure us that Jesus' blood paid our sin debt in full. When we confess "Jesus is Lord," and believe in our hearts that God raised Him from the dead, we will be saved (see Romans 10:9-10). Not only do Jesus' death and resurrection reconcile us to God our Father, but His blood washes us whiter than snow (see Psalm 51:7) and cleanses our consciences, so that we will never be put to shame when we trust in Him (see Romans 9:33). We must not allow the devil to prod us to hold onto our shame. Instead, we must hold tightly to the truth and enjoy the freedom that the shedding of Jesus' blood so generously gives us.

Moreover, God Himself forgets our shortcomings and erases them from all of history. In Isaiah 43:25, the Lord says, "I, even I, am He Who blots out your transgressions, for My own sake, and remembers your sins no more." Hebrews 10:15-18 says:

> The Holy Spirit also testifies to us about this. First He says:

> "This is the covenant I will make with them after that time, says the Lord. I will put my laws in their hearts, and I will write them on their minds."
>
> Then He adds:
>
> *"Their sins and lawless acts I will remember no more."*
>
> *And where these have been forgiven, there is no longer any sacrifice for sin.* (Emphasis mine)

If Jesus Christ paid your sin debt once for all and God no longer remembers your sin, why should you? Do not allow Satan to hold power over your conscience. You are a new creation in Christ Jesus; "the old has gone, the new has come!" (See 2 Corinthians 5:17) Let the Holy Spirit renew your mind with the mind and thoughts of God. Claim these powerful verses for yourself:

> Hide Your face from my sins and blot out all my iniquity. Create in me a pure heart, O God, and renew a steadfast spirit within me. Do not cast me from Your presence or take Your Holy Spirit from me. Restore to me the joy of Your salvation and grant me a willing spirit, to sustain me. (Psalm 51:9-12)

I pray that God will restore to you the joy of His salvation so you may claim victory over your sin and shame, living in the freedom purchased for you by the blood of Christ. Do not minimize the result of Jesus' sacrifice in your life. It is no small thing! Use the following verses to remind yourself that you have been redeemed by the blood of Jesus Christ. Don't let the devil repeatedly condemn you with memories of your past sin, guilt, and shame. It has been wiped out by God; it's gone forever!

The Truth in God's Word:

"Come now, let us reason together," says the Lord. "Though your sins are like scarlet, they shall be as white as snow; though they are red as crimson, they shall be like wool." (Isaiah 1:18)

Everyone who sins breaks the law; in fact, sin is lawlessness. But you know that He appeared so that He might take away our sins. And in Him is no sin. No one who lives in Him keeps on sinning. No one who continues to sin has either seen Him or known Him...No one who is born of God will continue to sin, because God's seed remains in him; he cannot go on sinning, because he has been born of God. (1 John 3:4-6, 9)

This is what the Lord says—your Redeemer, the Holy One of Israel... "Forget the former things; do not dwell on the past. See, I am doing a new thing! Now it springs up; do you not perceive it? (Isaiah 43:1, 18-19)

This is what the Lord says, "For I will forgive their wickedness and will remember their sins no more." (Jeremiah 31:34)

Therefore, if anyone is in Christ, he is a new creation; the old has gone, the new has come! All this is from God, Who reconciled us to Himself through Christ and gave us the ministry of reconciliation: that God was reconciling the world to Himself in Christ, *not counting men's sins against them.* And He has committed to us the message of reconciliation. We are therefore Christ's ambassadors, as though God were making His appeal through us. We implore you on Christ's behalf: Be reconciled to God. God made Him Who had no sin to be sin for us, so that in Him we might become the righteousness of God. (2 Corinthians 5:17-21; emphasis mine)

LIE #3: God will *never* speak to you because of your sin or past.

Never is a long time. *Never* is one of those definitive words that completely eliminates all possibilities of something happening. It's true God hides His face from sin, and our sin separates us from God. When repetitive sin holds you in its grip, God may choose not to listen to you or speak to you for a time. God does not reward disobedience with the ability to hear His voice.

When our iniquities separate us from God and our sins cause God to hide His face from us, He will not hear us, and chances are He won't speak to us either. However, when we find our way back to Him through confession and repentance, it greatly reduces the distance from us to never. The Father welcomes the lost sinner; in fact, He throws a feast of celebration when the lost is found (see Luke 15:23).

TRUTH #3: God speaks to His children.

If you have confessed Jesus as your Savior and Lord, you already possess everything you need to hear His voice—the Holy Spirit dwelling in you. Being perfect and sin-free are not prerequisites to hearing from God. If that were true, nobody would ever hear His voice. However, when you do not confess your sin and repent, or turn from it, then you are not living in step with the Spirit and allowing the Spirit to take the lead role in your life.

When you are filled with the Spirit and controlled by the Spirit, you will feel the Spirit's conviction immediately following disobedience. Even better, you will sense the Holy Spirit leading you away from sin before it happens. He encourages your obedience to God's commands and discourages your intention to commit unrighteous offenses.

When we delay our confession, repentance, and plea for forgiveness for our sin against God and others, the sin proliferates into disobedience. We rebel against God any time we do not obey Him or His commands.

Repetitive sin is difficult to throw off in our own strength, but when we rely on the strength of the Holy Spirit, He empowers us to resist temptation, continuously develops our Christ-like behavior, and perfects our faith. Hebrews 12:1-6 says:

> Therefore, since we are surrounded by such a great cloud of witnesses, let us throw off everything that hinders and the sin that so easily entangles, and let us run with perseverance the race marked out for us. Let us fix our eyes on Jesus, the author and perfecter of our faith, who for the joy set before Him endured the cross, scorning its shame, and sat down at the right hand of the throne of God. Consider Him who endured such opposition from sinful men, so that you will not grow weary and lose heart.
> In your struggle against sin, you have not yet resisted to the point of shedding your blood. And you have forgotten that word of encouragement that addresses you as sons:
>
>> "My son, do not make light of the Lord's discipline, and do not lose heart when He rebukes you, because the Lord disciplines those He loves, and He punishes everyone He accepts as a son" (Proverbs 3:11-12).

As a new creation in Jesus Christ, your old way of living is gone, and the new way of living is *hear* (misspelling of the word "here" is intentional). Your new attitudes and actions are inspired by *hear*ing and obeying the voice of the Holy Spirit within you. Dr. Charles F. Stanley[21] says:

> God wants to speak to us if we're willing to quietly listen for the Holy Spirit's inaudible voice. Sometimes during prayer, He may lay something on

---

[21] Dr. Charles F. Stanley, *What Does Obedience Require?* (InTouch Ministries, intouch.org, Sermon Notes SN150823, 2016).

our heart or give us a sense of direction regarding a decision we must make. However, the Lord never tells us anything that contradicts His Word. That's why meditation on the Scriptures is essential. It's our source of guidance, comfort, and strength. If a particular passage grabs our attention, we should pause and ask the Lord if He's trying to tell us something. Then as we meditate on those verses, God will begin to shape our minds to think the way He does.

Obedience can be defined as doing what God says, how He says, and when He says to do it…He always enables us to do whatever He requires.

Full obedience to God requires completing His will, in His timing, in His way, and anything less or different is still disobedience and rebellion. Partial obedience does not deserve the full measure of blessings from God. Negative consequences are attached to anything other than full obedience. As a result of our disobedience and out of God's great love for us, He disciplines us to protect us and teach us obedience in the future. When we obey God's commands and instructions, His best blessings are in store for us.

To hear God's voice, we must demonstrate our obedience to His will. At the same time, when we do not yet hear His voice, our obedience depends on what we know of His Word. But when we sin, we feel the conviction of the Holy Spirit by hearing His voice within us, encouraging us to make the right decisions and choose the correct paths. The best way to live in obedience to God is to read His Word every day and make time to listen to His voice at least every morning, if not throughout the entire day. The more we train ourselves to be in tune to His voice all day long, the better we are able to live every moment in the Spirit rather than in the flesh.

Listening to God means fully obeying Him—that is, doing what He says, how He says, when He says. Choosing not to obey God when we hear Him may cause God to stop speaking to us for a period of time. The children of Israel heard God's word, but they repeatedly ignored and disobeyed it, so God finally quit speaking to them. When we do not follow through on all the aspects of His message to us, He may choose to move on and speak to someone who will listen *and* obey.

When we hear God's voice and follow His instructions, we have access to the power of God's Spirit within us. It's no wonder Satan doesn't want us to listen to God's voice. We become a huge threat to the devil's work when we are tuned in to God and living in a sweet, intimate relationship with Jesus Christ by the power of the Holy Spirit. God pursues and rewards people who listen to His voice, hear His Word, and obey it.

When we accept Christ as our Savior and receive the Holy Spirit in our hearts, we should allow Him to work in us. As we yield ourselves to God's Spirit within us, He leads us in the sanctification process of becoming more like Christ. As we try to live a life that pleases God, we become closer to God. The more intimate our relationship with God, the better we can hear Him speak. "Those who live according to the sinful nature have their minds set on what that nature desires; but those who live in accordance with the Spirit have their minds set on what the Spirit desires. The mind of sinful man is death, but the mind controlled by the Spirit is life and peace" (Romans 8:5-6).

Furthermore, in addressing Lie #2 above, we established that when you ask God's forgiveness for your sins, not only does He forgive you, He blots them out and remembers them no more. So if you live life with a contrite heart, you will confess your sin when convicted by the Holy Spirit, and, in His power, repent and change your ways. Therefore, we may conclude that God does not always avoid conversation with you because of your sin, present or past. As long as you do not live in repetitive or blatant disobedience, you can hear His voice if you maintain a good relationship with Him, listening to *and* obeying Him.

Still, it's easy to believe the enemy's false whispers. I know, because I myself live it. To my regret, too many times the roaring lion catches me off guard and causes me to believe God is disappointed in me or distant from me because of my sin, my past, or even my lack of attentiveness to Him. It requires a constant awareness of the presence of evil and the authoritative power of Jesus Christ to overcome these lies with the truth of God's Word: I am a child of God—I belong to God—therefore, I will hear Him speak (see John 8:47). The truth is, whenever I have distanced myself from God and then returned to Him as a repentant child, He runs out to greet me with open arms because He longs to resume communication with me again.

Holding onto the past leaves us in bondage. God sent Jesus to proclaim freedom for the captives (see Isaiah 61:1-3). Live in the freedom Christ has to offer, so that you can worship God with all your heart and hear God's voice clearly. Clinging to your past, or your past sins, can keep you from hearing the voice of God. Let go of your past. Do the work you need to do to move on. Seek God's forgiveness and healing, and then let it go—God does.

"It is for freedom that Christ has set us free. Stand firm, then, and do not let yourselves be burdened again by a yoke of slavery" (Galatians 5:1). To better illustrate this verse, picture a yoke of oxen. Two animals are harnessed together so that they will make better progress. When one gets weak and tired, the other remains strong. They support each other. One can rest while the other carries the burden. On the other hand, a yoke also ties them together for a time, like two people who are handcuffed to each other. There is no getting away from the other unless you have the key to unlock the shackles.

A yoke has room for only two. You can be yoked with Satan or you can be yoked with Jesus. Being yoked with the enemy means being held in slavery to Satan and sin. It means spending an eternity apart from God. But when you are connected with Jesus, He gives you rest, carries you when you are weak, and leads you on a path to an eternal presence with God. He takes the emotional baggage you lug around with you and trades it for a lighter load. You can rest in

Him as He removes the weight that impedes you. You may experience God's peace even in the midst of the storms of life.

Jesus took my yoke of slavery—the poor choices, past sins, shame, and lies I held tightly—and exchanged my heavy burden for an easier yoke with Him. He lightened my load, carried my excess baggage, and gave me rest. He traded my senseless life of oppression for an uninhibited life of freedom and peace in Him. He liberated me and released me from the burden of the past. This new freedom allowed me to know and hear His voice clearly. So I claim this verse: "My soul finds rest in God alone; my salvation comes from Him. He alone is my rock and my salvation; He is my fortress, I will never be shaken" (Psalm 62:1-2).

The Truth in God's Word

Jesus said to them, "He who belongs to God hears what God says." (John 8:47)

The Man who enters by the gate is the Shepherd of His sheep. The watchman opens the gate for Him, and *the sheep listen to His voice.* He calls His own sheep by name and leads them out. When He has brought out all His own, He goes on ahead of them, and *His sheep follow Him because they know His voice.* (John 10:2-4; emphasis mine with italicized phrases and capitalized nouns and pronouns in reference to God)

This day I call heaven and earth as witnesses against you that I have set before you life and death, blessings and curses. Now choose life, so that you and your children may live and that you may love the

Lord your God, *listen to His voice*, and hold fast to Him. (Deuteronomy 30:19-20; emphasis mine)

The Sovereign Lord has given me an instructed tongue, to know the word that sustains the weary. He wakens me morning by morning, *wakens my ear to listen like one being taught.* The Sovereign Lord has opened my ears, and I have not been rebellious; I have not drawn back. (Isaiah 50:4-5; emphasis mine)

"Here I am! I stand at the door and knock. If anyone *hears My voice* and opens the door, I will come in and eat with him, and he with Me." (Revelation 3:20; emphasis mine)

"My sheep listen to My voice; I know them, and they follow Me." (John 10:27)

"We know that God does not listen to sinners. He listens to the godly man who does His will." (John 9:31)

Next, read about God's heart on disobedience, as He communicated to me in four **Manna for Today** excerpts.

"All the prophets testify about Him that everyone who believes in Him receives forgiveness of sins through His name" (Acts 10:43).

Forgiver[22]

Do you believe in Me? When you confess your sins and believe in Me, you are forgiven. Your sins have been pardoned. You have been excused from the death sentence. The wages of sin is death, but I paid your debt on the cross. You have been exonerated in My name. Your slate has been wiped clean. I have blotted out all your transgressions. The great chasm that once separated you from God has been bridged by My obedience to God's will, even unto death.

I died so that you would be forgiven and reconciled to your heavenly Father. Now you must also forgive those who trespass against you. Your debt was great, but it has been paid. Forgive the debts of those who sin against you; and your heavenly Father will forgive you; but when you do not forgive men their sins, your Father in heaven will not forgive you of your sins. How many times have I forgiven you? In turn, you must forgive your brother time and time again. If you forgive anyone, My Father also forgives him.

In Me you have redemption. You have been delivered from your sins. Do not be bound by sin and temptation. Repent of your sin and be free from all temptation, for I will provide the way out. Find your freedom in Me. Turn away from your wicked ways, and become the new creature I have designed you to be. Your sins have been forgiven. You have been washed clean. You will trade in your filthy rags for My robe of righteousness.

I love you so much that I laid My life down for yours. You are My child, My beloved bride. You are now without spot or blemish. You have been made clean in My name. Forgive others as you have been forgiven. Do not hold onto the sins that have already been forgiven in My name. Let go of the misdeeds from your past, and find freedom in My forgiveness.

✝

---

[22] Sindy Nagel, "Forgiver" in *Manna for Today: Bread from Heaven for Each Day* (Bloomington, IN: WestBow Press 2012), 136.

It is for freedom that Christ has set us free. Stand firm, then, and do not let yourselves be burdened again by a yoke of slavery (Galatians 5:1).

I Have Set You Free[23]

At one time you were held in captivity, bound by the chains around your neck. You were a prisoner of the enemy who seeks to destroy you because you are Mine. You once were enslaved by the thoughts My adversary forced upon you. Behold, I came to release you from your bondage. It is for freedom that I have set you free. Do not take upon yourself the opponent's yoke of slavery again. I have overcome the enemy of your soul. I declare the victory in the battle for your heart. You are My child; you belong to Me.

Once you walked in darkness, but now you have seen the light. I am the light of the world shining before all men. I pierce the darkness with My sword. The darkness gives way to the light. I am the truth, and the truth shall set you free. I have revealed the deceitful ways of your captor. Never again should you live within the prison walls he sets up before you. You have tasted the sweetness of liberty. Be wise. Do not forget the One who has set you free.
I will not render you helpless. You hold My power in your hands. Remain alert, and prepare for the battle. Know My Word, and use it as your weapon. It will stop your enemy in his tracks. Nothing can penetrate like the Word of God. Put on My suit of armor; it will protect your heart and mind. Worship Me in gladness, and ward away all evil.

Remember it is for freedom that I have set you free. Protect yourself from the slavery of sin. Do not return to your former ways. You are a new creation. The old has passed away, and the new is yet to come. Walk in the narrow way, and do not depart from it. Keep your focus on the prize I have set before you, and do not look back. Live in the freedom I have provided for you. It did not come without a price. I paid it willingly for your sake. Remain in Me, and maintain the liberation of your soul.

✝

---

[23] Sindy Nagel, "I Have Set You Free" in *Manna for Today: Bread from Heaven for Each Day* (Bloomington, IN: WestBow Press 2012), 147.

"This is the covenant I will make with them after that time, says the Lord. I will put My laws in their hearts, and I will write them on their minds." Then He adds: "Their sins and lawless acts I will remember no more." And where these have been forgiven, there is no longer any sacrifice for sin (Hebrews 10:16-18).

Divine Dementia[24]

I have chosen to forget your ways. I no longer remember your sins and lawlessness. You have been forgiven. Your debt was paid at the cross. I replace the evil devices in your heart and mind with My laws and commandments. This is My promise to you. You have been forgiven. You are My child. You belong to Me. You will not suffer the sacrifice for your sin. Jesus paid the ultimate price on the cross—once for all—once for you. You have been redeemed. You are a new creation in Christ Jesus. The old is gone, the new is here.

Now you must choose the same. Forget your old ways. Do not torment yourself with memories of your past sin. I have wiped clean your slate. There is no room for shame when your heart has been redeemed by Me. I release you from your guilt. I free you from your disgrace. I have replaced your remorse with honor and righteousness. You are justified by My grace. Your name is written in the book of life. You will spend eternity with Me.

Your obedience is My joy. Remember My laws. I have written them on your mind. I have put them in your heart. Abide by them. Your life will be long and prosperous. You will experience the joy of My salvation when you conform to My ways. Listen for My voice in your heart. You know My voice. Act upon My directions. I have mapped out the best possible road for you to travel upon. I will not lead you astray. Be willing to change your course when necessary. I know what is in your best interest. I will prosper you. You will live a full life in the abundance I have planned for you. Delight yourself in Me. I give you the desires of your heart. Stay close to Me. I will never leave your side. Trust Me with your life. You may depend on Me. I will provide all that you ever need. Remain in Me, and I will remain in you.

✝

---

[24] Sindy Nagel, "Divine Dementia" in *Manna for Today: Bread from Heaven for Each Day* (Bloomington, IN: WestBow Press 2012), 153.

But God demonstrates His own love for us in this: While we were still sinners, Christ died for us (Romans 5:8).

Christ Died for You[25]

I love you, My child. I demonstrated My love for you by sending My Son to die for you—not just death, but death on a cross. Jesus Christ paid the ultimate price for your sin. While you were still powerless, He sacrificed Himself for you. He gave His life in exchange for yours. As a result of His death, you have received reconciliation with Me. Will you come to Me?

You were born into the sin of Adam, but you have been made righteous through the obedience of Christ. Do not go on sinning then, when you have been baptized into Christ. You must die to your sin, as you have died and been buried with Christ. If you have died with Christ, you will also live again with Him. No longer are you a slave to your sin. You have been freed from your sin through the death and resurrection of Jesus Christ. Count yourself, then, as dead to sin, but alive to God in Christ.

Do not be sold out to sin, but be sold out to life in Me. There is a life to which you can obtain the freedom of righteousness. A life made free through the righteousness of Christ, is a life made free from sin and death. Live your life in obedience to Me, just as Christ was obedient to Me. Turn away from the life that calls you into unrighteousness. Stand up for what you believe in, and live a life of freedom.

I have loved you with a sacrificial love. I gave My Son's life for you. Will you now live for Me? Live a life that is pleasing to Me. Do not continue in self-indulgence, but indulge yourself in Me. I am worthy of your time and energy. I will empower you to live into your freedom, the freedom that I give you. You are not bound by the chains of imprisonment. You have been set free. You are free to live your life accomplishing My work. I have created you to carry out My will. My plans are to prosper you. My plans are perfect. Live in the excellence of My will. I know what is best for you. My ways are higher than your ways. Your ways have not brought you the happiness that you seek. Abandon your ways. Live according to My will, and the joy of obedience will

---

[25] Sindy Nagel, "Christ Died for You" in *Manna for Today: Bread from Heaven for Each Day* (Bloomington, IN: WestBow Press 2012), 11.

fill your heart. I love you, and I want the best for you. I am the best thing that will ever happen to you. Believe Me.

Self-Reflection:

1. Define disobedience to God, and give a recent example of your disobedience to Him.

2. When your child breaks your rules, your pet disobeys, or someone under your authority does not follow orders, how do you correct or discipline their disobedience?

3. Does God punish our sin even though Jesus Christ paid the penalty for it? If so, how do you think this is accomplished? How has God disciplined you for your wrongdoing?

4. Describe a way you may have put a limit on God's forgiveness in the past.

5. How aware are you of the battle going on in your mind? Do you recognize when Satan tries to tempt you, mislead you, deceive you, confuse you, or condemn you? Give examples of ways the devil plays you and how you respond:

6. What does full obedience to God require?

7. List a couple reasons why we should forget our sin after we have confessed it and repented from it:

Removing the Barrier of Disobedience

Ask God to expose the lies and help you identify any false beliefs that cause a barrier of disobedience between you and God. Record them here.

Request that God bring memories to your mind of His presence in your life as it relates to your struggles with disobedience. Pay close attention to what He is doing and saying to you in your thoughts. Write it down here.

Allow the Holy Spirit to lead you to Scripture verses that shine the light of God's truth into the deceptions you've believed. The concordance in your Bible comes in handy when you're searching for verses regarding a topic or word you hear from the Lord. Write the Bible verses and references here.

In the power given to you by Jesus Christ, through the shedding of His blood, take authority over the enemy and his attempts to distract and confuse you with his misconceptions. Speak out loud to rebuke the devil and proclaim the truth of God's Word, which you recorded above.

Pray:

Heavenly Father, in Your Word, You give me commandments and instructions for obedient living. Please forgive me for falling prey to Satan's lies and temptations and acting in disobedience to You. Help me tune into Your Holy Spirit for direction in my daily activities and respond to His conviction and encouragement to do better. You love me so much You do not spare me the rod of correction when I stray.

I pray that I will learn obedience from the discipline You give me. Help me understand the full measure of Your love and forgiveness, gratefully accepting all of it. As Your Word promises, please blot out my transgressions and remember them no more. I ask for sharpness and alertness for the battle in my mind. Lord, I pray the Holy Spirit will help me recognize when the devil subtly influences my thoughts and my beliefs. Strengthen me for the battle and grant me Your wisdom, power, and authority over my enemy. Father, I desire to be obedient to You. Please show me what full obedience requires. I desire to hear Your voice within. Please do the work in me that is necessary to open the channels of communication with You. I submit myself to your Lordship. I pray in Jesus' name. Amen.

Listen:

Lord, what do You want me to know about my disobedience? (Write down all your thoughts and identify which thoughts may actually be God's voice.)

Chapter 7

Unwillingness to Forgive
The Enemy of Mercy

"And when you stand praying, if you hold anything against anyone, forgive him, so that your Father in heaven may forgive you your sins." (Mark 11:25)

It is one of the greatest gifts you can give yourself, to forgive. Forgive everybody.—Maya Angelou

From God's Heart to Yours

My precious child, extending mercy and forgiveness is not easy, I know. However, it is necessary for your spiritual growth and freedom. I ask only that you are as merciful and forgiving of others as I have been with you. Your sin and lawlessness deserved death. However, I gave My Son's life in exchange for yours. I do not ask you to do anything I have not already done for you. Will you lay down your life for the one who sinned against you? Will you lay down all anger, bitterness, and pride, offering your grace, mercy, and forgiveness instead?

You have been given much; therefore, much will be required of you. You have been forgiven much; therefore, you must also forgive much. Even though your sin debt was paid in full already, I still require that you forgive others before I will forgive you again and again. Repentance is required in order to receive My forgiveness. Forgiveness is required in order to maintain intimacy with Me. When you harbor an unforgiving spirit, you erect a barricade between us. What will bring down this wall? Your willingness to forgive.

Impossible? In your own power, yes. But by My Spirit, you can do all things. Seek Me for the necessary healing of your wounds. I will shine a light into the darkness. I will expose the lies and trade them for the truth. My truth will set you free from that which holds you captive.

It is difficult to extend mercy to the one who deeply wounded you, but walk in the Spirit rather than the flesh. My grace is sufficient for you. My power is upon you. In your weakness, you are strong. You are made in My image. I am a merciful God; that means you are full of mercy also. Draw from My deep well of forbearance and bless the one who hurt you. I can see the walls coming down already. Can you hear Me now?

UNWILLINGNESS TO FORGIVE

"For if you forgive men when they sin against you, your heavenly Father will also forgive you. But if you do not forgive men their sins, your Father will not forgive your sins" (Matthew 6:14-15).

God's Word is very clear on forgiveness. When we forgive others, God forgives us. When we do not forgive others, God does not forgive us. If we have an unforgiving heart, we put a distance between Him and ourselves. His voice may become silent. God may choose not to speak to us until we choose to forgive another who has hurt, offended, or sinned against us. A harsh, unforgiving, judgmental spirit can stifle our communication with God.

"Do not judge, and you will not be judged. Do not condemn, and you will not be condemned. Forgive, and you will be forgiven" (Luke 6:37). Again, we hear very clearly that God will forgive us when we forgive others. Sometimes it feels impossible to forgive someone who hurts us deeply. Truly, we cannot climb this mountain in our own strength. Just as the Holy Spirit gives us the power of self-control to abstain from sin and wrongdoing, He also gives us the ability to forgive. Asking the Holy Spirit to change your heart toward the person who offended you enables you to see that person through the eyes of God. Praying for your enemies also softens your heart for them. Begin with small, one-sentence prayers led by the Holy Spirit, and soon your blossoming mercy will increase your petitions on behalf of those who hurt you.

The Holy Spirit intercedes for us when we do not know what to pray. Tune in to the Spirit of God within you to receive power from on high to do what seems impossible in your own strength. When you forgive others, God forgives you. When God forgives you, you must believe it and fully accept His gift of forgiveness. (See the previous chapter.)

Understanding how great a debt I owe for my sin and how much Jesus paid for it, I am grateful that God has already forgiven me. In turn, I should extend my gift of forgiveness to those who have sinned against me. Exercising forgiveness is a choice, just as *accepting* forgiveness is a choice.

> Therefore, as God's chosen people, holy and dearly loved, clothe yourselves with compassion, kindness, humility, gentleness and patience. Bear with each other and forgive whatever grievances you may have against one another. Forgive as the Lord forgave you. And over all these virtues put on love, which binds them all together in perfect unity. (Colossians 3:12-14)

Continually thank God for His forgiveness and ask Him to carry on the healing process in you, so you *feel* both forgiven and forgiving, then walk in the freedom that brings. When you are freed from an unforgiving heart and let go of the sin that holds onto you, you may hear God speak to you clearly. Until then, you may have to sift through a few lies to get to His truth.

LIE #1: I can't forgive my brother or sister—he/she hurt me too deeply.

The above statement would be true if you relied on your own strength to forgive your offender. However, as a child of God, you have the indwelling Holy Spirit to help you carry out the Christ-like behavior required of you in your sanctification process. Forgiving someone who hurt you deeply does not mean that you renounce your pain or excuse the behavior that caused it. It does mean, however, that you are choosing to release that person from the debt of the sin committed against you. Forgiveness is a choice. You may not *feel* like you have forgiven that person, but the feeling will eventually follow the action as you pray that God will liberate you from all anger, bitterness, disappointment, resentment, blame, and condemnation associated with the offense. The more often you pray for the person who offended you, the more the grudge grip lets go of you.

Forgiveness is still possible even when your offender doesn't request it or offer an apology for the wrongdoing. He/she may not even realize that his/her actions caused you any pain. I remember

Jesus' example of this as He hung on the cross and said, "Father, forgive them, for they do not know what they are doing" (Luke 23:34). Jesus led a life of obedience to His heavenly Father. He committed no sins. Yet He was crucified for the sins—past, present, and future—committed by every other person on earth. He bore the weight of all our sin, and still He extended mercy to those who beat Him, mocked Him, spat on Him, and hung Him on a tree.

When we confess our sin and accept Jesus as our Savior, God forgives us for all our past sins. This includes offenses which we may have committed in ignorance. At the time of our spiritual rebirth, our collective past sins are so numerous, we don't usually confess them one by one. We may not even realize when we have been rebellious, offensive, hurtful, or disobedient. We may not know when we have hurt someone. But forgiveness is a gift that was purchased by the death of God's one and only Son, Jesus Christ. His grace and forgiveness are FREE gifts available to us. In turn, we too can freely forgive someone who has not asked for it. Ephesians 4:32 says, "Be kind and compassionate to one another, forgiving each other, just as in Christ God forgave you."

Almost always, forgiveness benefits the giver much more than the receiver. When we forgive someone, we release them from the debt incurred by their misconduct. While it seems the offender is getting off without penalty, the forgiver will experience greater freedom because the chains of bondage caused by an unforgiving spirit are broken. Many times, we are torn up inside for years over a misdeed done to us, while the offender pays no penalty and carries no remorse for the damage he/she caused. But forgiving him/her releases the heavy burden that we carry, liberating us to enjoy a closer, more intimate relationship with our Savior and Lord. Forgiveness is for the forgiver.

TRUTH
#1: With God all things are possible.

At times it seems impossible to extend forgiveness to someone who has profoundly hurt us emotionally, physically, or spiritually through his/her actions or words. Truly, forgiving someone who has severely wounded us cannot be accomplished in our own strength. When pain cuts deeply into our souls, we become emotionally disabled. Our fleshly desires of retaliation and revenge seep into our thoughts, prolonging the heartache. Dealing with the anguish in an emotionally healthy manner requires more than is humanly possible. Claim this verse from Philippians 4:13 for yourself, "I can do everything through Him [Christ] who gives me strength."

Read "The Parable of the Unmerciful Servant" in Matthew 18:21-35. Peter asked Jesus, "Lord, how many times shall I forgive my brother when he sins against me? Up to seven times?" Jesus answered, "I tell you, not seven times, but seventy-seven times." Then He likened the kingdom of heaven to a king who wanted to settle accounts with his servants. A servant owed the king a sum of money equal to several million dollars. The man was not able to pay, so the master ordered that the man, his wife, and all his children be sold to repay the debt. The servant pleaded with him, asking for patience until he could repay everything. The master took pity on him, canceled the debt, and let him go. But then that same servant found one of his fellow servants, who owed him a few dollars. He began to choke him and demanded that he immediately pay back what he owed. His fellow servant fell to his knees, begging him to have patience, but the first servant refused. Instead, he had the man thrown into prison until he could repay the debt. The other servants were greatly distressed and reported this to the master. The master called in the first servant and said, "You wicked servant, I canceled all that debt of yours because you begged me to. Shouldn't you have had mercy on your fellow servant just as I had on you?" Then the angry master turned him over to the jailers until he could repay all he owed. Jesus concluded, "This is how my heavenly Father will treat each of you unless you forgive your brother or sister from your heart."

God requires that we forgive our debtors. When that expectation is much too difficult for us to accomplish on our own, we can tap into the power of God's Holy Spirit within us. The Spirit helps us in our weakness and empowers us to do that which seems impossible on our own. It's all part of the process of becoming more

Christ-like. It's necessary to be obedient to the will of our heavenly Father and to maintain unhindered communication with Him.

The Truth in God's Word:

Again Jesus said, "Peace be with you! As the Father has sent Me, I am sending you." And with that He breathed on them and said, "Receive the Holy Spirit. If you forgive anyone his sins, they are forgiven; if you do not forgive them, they are not forgiven." (John 20:21-23)

If you forgive anyone, I also forgive him. And what I have forgiven—if there was anything to forgive—I have forgiven in the sight of Christ for your sake, in order that Satan might not outwit us. For we are not unaware of his schemes. (2 Corinthians 2:10-11)

"Forgive us our debts, as we have also forgiven our debtors." (Matthew 6:12)

If we claim to be without sin, we deceive ourselves and the truth is not in us. If we confess our sins, He is faithful and just and will forgive us our sins and purify us from all unrighteousness. If we claim we have not sinned, we make Him out to be a liar and His word has no place in our lives. (1 John 1:8-10)

You are kind and forgiving, O Lord, abounding in love to all who call to you. (Psalm 86:5)

LIE #2: God doesn't expect me to forgive this one.

I recognize a loss for exactly the right words to address this tough subject. I know that some sins committed against us, and some of the people who committed these offenses, seem too painful and awful to forgive. The wounds run too deep to heal or get past. And when these offenses have been perpetrated against us over and over for months or years, the debt seems insurmountable and the violation impossible to pardon. However, this is exactly what Jesus asks us to do.

TRUTH #2: God requires that we forgive *all* those who trespass against us.

Forgive anyone of anything. Forgive everyone of everything. Those are difficult words to digest, let alone practice. Still, it's exactly what Jesus taught. In Mark 11:25, Jesus says, "And when you stand praying, if you hold *anything against anyone*, forgive him, so that your Father in heaven may forgive you your sins" (emphasis mine).

Look at the italicized AAA words in the above verse: *Anything Against Anyone*. That pretty well sums it up. We must release our hold on *anything* (everything) done by *anyone* (everyone). No exclusions. No exceptions. There is no fine print that precludes us from obeying God on this point.

The amazing reward we receive when we release these debts from our debtors is FREEDOM—emotional, physical, and spiritual. Letting go of the unrelenting emotional strain of constantly reliving the wound frees up space in your mind for more positive thoughts and memories. Bitterness can manifest in many different physical problems and maladies. Inhibiting spiritual growth runs alongside the emotional and physical effects of harboring an unforgiving heart.

"Now the Lord is the Spirit, and where the Spirit of the Lord is, there is freedom. And we, who with unveiled faces all reflect the Lord's glory, are being transformed into His likeness with ever-increasing glory, which comes from the Lord, Who is the Spirit" (2 Corinthians 3:17-18). As a child of God, you have received His Spirit and freedom, because the Spirit is transforming you into the likeness of Jesus. And Jesus desires that we forgive others as He has forgiven us. He has single-handedly provided the way for *anyone* to be forgiven of *anything*.

"It is for freedom that Christ has set us free. Stand firm, then, and do not let yourselves be burdened again by a yoke of slavery" (Galatians 5:1). Any trespass against us that we don't consciously and intentionally release becomes a yoke of slavery, a prison we occupy. The key that will open the door of our jail cell is the action of extending the same mercy God has shown us to the one who trespassed against us. Reclaim a life of freedom for yourself by forgiving, with God's help, *everyone* for *everything* before they ever ask.

Colossians 3:13 says, "Bear with each other and forgive *whatever* grievances you may have against one another. Forgive as the Lord forgave you" (emphasis mine). The italicized word *whatever* means just that—anything and everything. Almighty God does not ask us to do that which He has not already done Himself. He chose to send His only Son, Jesus, to redeem us from our sin debt. He provided the path for our forgiveness and reconciliation in Him. That was no small gesture. Our lives are forever changed as a result of Jesus' sacrifice.

In Matthew 6:9-15, the Lord's Prayer, Jesus models how to pray to accomplish the Father's good will and pleasure.

> "This, then, is how you should pray:
>
> "'Our Father in heaven, hallowed be Your name, Your kingdom come, Your will be done, on earth as it is in heaven. Give us today our daily bread. Forgive us our debts, as we also have forgiven our debtors. And lead us not into temptation, but deliver us from the evil one.'
>
> "For if you forgive men when they sin against you, your heavenly Father will also forgive you. But if you do not forgive men their sins, your Father will not forgive your sins."

Do you see how an unforgiving heart establishes and maintains an obstruction to intimacy with God? Allowing your heart to harden toward anyone destroys the image of God in you. It shows blatant disrespect for your relationship with the Lord, as well as willful disobedience to God's perfect will and plan for your life. And yet it requires complete submission of your broken spirit to the leadership of God's Holy Spirit within you to forgive those who have severely wounded you. Sometimes it forces you to revisit and examine your unpleasant emotional pain, while seeking the healing transformation only God can perform in your heart.

I feel blessed to have experienced God's divine inner healing in my own heart through a method called Transformation Prayer Ministry (TPM). My depression counselor was an experienced facilitator in this process and ushered me into the care of Jesus through Transformation Prayer sessions. If you are interested in learning more about Transformation Prayer Ministry, see the TPM website at www.transformationprayer.org. At the time of this publication, the ministry was updating its online training, making it not only an effective method used by counselors, but also a "way of life" to be used daily by every Christ follower.

Another excellent resource for inner healing prayer is the Northwest Gathering Center in Coeur d'Alene, Idaho, founded by Bill and Sue Frisbie. They were trained and served on the staff of Elijah House Ministries for years. Their passion is to help others

TRUTH #3: God will forgive you *after* you forgive others.

In the verses following the Lord's Prayer, Jesus explicitly states God's stance on how to be forgiven:

> "For if you forgive men when they sin against you, your heavenly Father will also forgive you. But if you do not forgive men their sins, your Father will not forgive your sins." (Matthew 6:14-15)

Redundantly, both in the Lord's Prayer and in the verses that follow, Jesus stated that we must forgive others *before* the heavenly Father will forgive us. When we don't forgive others, God does not forgive us. That is seriously simple and scary: Forgive and be forgiven; do not forgive and you are not forgiven. I want my sins forgiven by God, so I *must* forgive others first. How often do we consider this? Forgiveness is not a feeling; it's a choice—a way of life. No further discussion necessary, right?

"Jesus looked at them and said, 'With man this is impossible, but with God all things are possible'" (Matthew 19:26). In the context of this verse, Jesus speaks about how we can be saved. However, we can apply it to forgiveness also because "with God *all* things are possible" (emphasis mine). Accordingly, Philippians 4:13 says, "I can do everything through Him Who gives me strength."

Chapter 7 – UNWILLINGNESS TO FORGIVE

Truth in God's Word:

"For if you forgive men when they sin against you, your heavenly Father will also forgive you. *But if you do not forgive men their sins, your Father will not forgive your sins.*" (Matthew 6:14-15; emphasis mine)

In the following *Manna for Today* excerpts, read God's words, which He spoke to me years ago. He doesn't always cut His instructions into bite-sized pieces for us to chew on and contemplate. Often, He firmly lays out direct orders for us, describing how we are to live in a Christ-like manner, doing so from the depth of His love for His creation and His desire that we experience fullness of life.

"Therefore I tell you, whatever you ask for in prayer, believe that you have received it, and it will be yours. And when you stand praying, if you hold anything against anyone, forgive him, so that your Father in heaven may forgive you your sins" (Mark 11:24-25).

No Room for Resentment [26]

My beloved one, come to Me in prayer. I love to hear you present your requests before Me. How is your faith? Do you believe I will give you what you ask for? Pray it, believe it, and receive it. Ask for anything in My name, believe it, and it will be yours; but if you pray while you hold on to resentment toward a brother or sister, your words will return empty. Do not conceal your bitterness. Do not harbor a grudge against anyone. Forgive the trespasses that offended you, so that I may forgive your trespasses that offend Me.

This is not a request. I instruct you out of the greatness of My heart. Your spiritual health is My first priority. Our relationship has to remain pure, unscathed by the sin of an unforgiving heart. You must forgive because you, yourself, have been forgiven. I bore the guilt of your sin. I died in your place. You will not suffer the sting of the death penalty. You have been excused from your sentence and reconciled to your Creator. I have pardoned your offenses.

You have been given the gift of new life, even life eternal. Extend the same grace to another—the forgiveness that I have extended to you. Holding onto resentment causes the most harm to the owner of it. Forgive your offender, and experience the freedom of letting go. It takes more effort to hold onto a grudge than it does to release it, but more importantly, My hands will not be tied by the power of your resentment. Sin causes a separation from Me that I despise. Please check your unforgiving spirit at the door. Do not approach Me until you have been reconciled to your brother. I will be waiting for you with great anticipation. I can't wait to be with you again. Listen to My instructions, and remove any obstacles between us. You'll be amazed at how good it feels. The possibilities are limitless. The feeling of freedom is worth the risk of letting go.

✝

---

[26] Sindy Nagel, "No Room for Resentment" in *Manna for Today: Bread from Heaven for Each Day* (Bloomington, IN: WestBow Press 2012), 65.

hear Me: Love your enemies, do good to those who hate
curse you, pray for those who mistreat you" (Luke 6:27-

Love Your Enemies[27]

My darling, you hear Me correctly. Love your enemies. Yes, I say love them, pray for them, bless them, do good things to them. When you do good things to your human opponents, your spiritual enemy, the devil, has no basis for attack. In loving your human enemy, she has no reason to hate you. When you bless her, her heart softens in My hand. Pray for her, and I will intercede for her. When you do these things, the anger and resentment you hold onto will fade away. As the bitterness fades away, loving your enemies will become easier.

See your adversary through My eyes. She is My child, too. I created her, just as I created you. The challenges that molded her in life may be different than your challenges. She has been wounded by her own enemies. Her heart has hardened in her own self-defense. Her responses to her ordeals may not be honoring to Me, but examine your own heart. Are you without fault?

As you pray for her, set your mind on the things above. You cannot do this in your own strength, but I am with you. When you do not have the words to pray, I will step in and help you. The one you oppose is My child too. Would you be the one to bring her back to Me? Would your actions be honoring to Me? Do you think more of Me than you do of yourself? Listen to My commands. Obey My teaching. Honor Me with your ways. Pray for your adversary, and bless her through Me. When you go against your own nature and love your enemies, your rewards will be great, both internally and eternally. Reap the benefits of My love when you love each other unconditionally as I have loved you.

✝

---

[27] Sindy Nagel, "Love Your Enemies" in *Manna for Today: Bread from Heaven for Each Day* (Bloomington, IN: WestBow Press 2012), 51.

Therefore, as God's chosen people, holy and dearly loved, clothe yourselves with compassion, kindness, humility, gentleness and patience. Bear with each other and forgive whatever grievances you may have against one another. Forgive as the Lord forgave you. And over all these virtues put on love, which binds them all together in perfect unity (Colossians 3:12-14).

Forgive as the Lord Forgave You[28]

You are one of My chosen people. I have set you apart. When you confessed Me as your Savior, you died to your former ways. You were crucified with Me. You live no more, but I live in you. Put to death any of your old earthly ways like: anger, rage, malice, filthy language, and lies. Put on your new self, which is being renewed in the image of your Creator. Therefore, be kind, compassionate, humble, gentle, and patient. This is the manner in which I lived while I was on the earth.

Live as one who is holy because you belong to Me. Be tolerant of each other, and forgive each other in all things. Forgive as you have been forgiven. Your Father in heaven does not hold anything against you. When you confess your sin, God forgives you without question. Your Father in heaven does not keep a record of wrongs. You must do the same. When you forgive someone, forget their misdeeds. Remember them no more. God, in His ultimate grace and mercy, has provided the way to forgiveness. If you forgive others of their sins, God will forgive you of yours; but if you do not forgive others of their sins, God will not forgive yours.

Above all things practice My love. This is the most desirable quality you have to give. Love will forgive a multitude of sins. Love binds all these things together in harmony. Do not love as the world does. Practice My love. Love does not fail. It is the most excellent way. If you have all these good features, and do not display My love, you are just making a loud noise. You have gained nothing; but when you put on My love to love another person, they will experience God Himself through His image bearer. Love as you have been loved. Forgive as the Lord forgave you.

✝

---

[28] Sindy Nagel, "Forgive as the Lord Forgave You" in *Manna for Today: Bread from Heaven for Each Day* (Bloomington, IN: WestBow Press 2012), 70.

Self-Reflection:

1. In your own words, describe what it means to forgive someone.

2. Compare your description of forgiveness with the Scripture passages about forgiveness discussed in this chapter. Are there any differences? Anything you missed or added?

3. Is there someone you know you need to forgive? Write their name(s) here.

4. How do you feel about extending forgiveness to someone even if they don't ask for it?

5. What is your understanding of forgiveness as it relates to the moment in time when you accepted Jesus Christ as your Savior? Were your sins forgiven then?

6. What is the relationship between your accepting the payment of Jesus dying on the cross for your sins and receiving God's forgiveness for your sins?

7. Consider this and write out your thoughts here: God forgave your sins when you accepted Jesus as your Savior. Why is God's future forgiveness now conditional upon your act of forgiving others? Support your answer with Scripture.

Removing the Barrier of an Unwillingness to Forgive

Ask God to expose the lies and help you identify any false beliefs that cause the barrier of an unwillingness to forgive between you and God. Record them here.

Request that God bring memories to your mind of His presence in your life as it relates to your struggles with an unwillingness to forgive. Pay close attention to what He is doing and saying to you in your thoughts. Write it down here.

Allow the Holy Spirit to lead you to Scripture verses that shine the light of God's truth into the deceptions you've believed. The concordance in your Bible comes in handy when you're searching for verses regarding a topic or word you hear from the Lord. Write the Bible verses and references here.

In the power given to you by Jesus Christ, through the shedding of His blood, take authority over the enemy and his attempts to distract and confuse you with his misconceptions. Speak out loud to rebuke the devil and proclaim the truth of God's Word, which you recorded above.

Pray:

Dear Father God, thank You for sending Your only Son, Jesus, to die in my place to pay the penalty for my sin. Your amazing grace provided the way for me to be spared from eternal separation from You. Thank You for the gift of the Holy Spirit, Who seals my inheritance of eternal life as Your child until the day of redemption. Please forgive my unwillingness to forgive others as you have forgiven me. I ask for Your help in this. I am made in the image of a merciful God. Please fill me with Your mercy toward those who have offended me and mistreated me. I release the anger, bitterness, and hatred that I feel toward my offender. I give it over to You and lift before You those who have hurt me. Help me extend mercy to those who have sinned against me. Please heal the deep hurt and pain I have held in my heart and replace it with Your perfect peace. Grant me freedom and release from the burden of an unforgiving spirit. I submit myself to You. Please break down the walls that kept me from hearing Your voice. I long to speak with You in intimate conversation. I ask this in the name of Jesus, my Savior and Lord. Amen.

Listen:

Lord, what do You want me to know about my unwillingness to forgive? (Write down all your thoughts and identify which thoughts may actually be God's voice.)

Conclusion

Are any of these seven roadblocks keeping you from experiencing intimacy with God and receiving all the wisdom and words God has for you? I hope you will take a few moments to consider each one and allow the Holy Spirit to convict you if you need to change your beliefs, philosophies, behaviors, or actions. Don't be overwhelmed if you relate to all seven. Choose one roadblock at a time, and ask the Holy Spirit to assist you in your healing and transformation. Then move on to the next. Don't wait until you have achieved excellence to listen to God. Instead, listen to God to achieve excellence.

In Jeremiah 33:3, God says, "Call to Me and I will answer you and tell you great and unsearchable things you do not know." When we call on God, He will answer us. I invite and encourage you to put God first in your life. Make time to meet with God alone and build a relationship with Him by knowing Him better and listening to His voice.

You have the risen Savior, Jesus Christ, living in you! Expect and believe God will speak to you! Don't be afraid of what He might say. Be more dependent on Him, and trust Him to meet all your needs. Set aside time each day to speak with God alone. Submit yourself to God and be obedient to His instructions. Forgive others as God forgave you. Annihilating these barriers will clear the path to two-way communication between God and you. Don't be surprised when you hear Him speaking to you. Hearing the voice of

God's Spirit within you is one of the keys to experiencing the abundant life Jesus Christ came to give you. Enjoy the freedom, peace, and confidence that intimate relationship with your Savior provides. Then be an inspiration to others when they see the image of Christ in your countenance and your character.

> In the love and service of Jesus Christ,
>
> *Sindy Nagel*
> Author/Speaker/Blogger

Thank You!

As a special "Thank you" gift, we are offering a free color .JPG file you can print and keep in your Quiet Time Journal as a reminder to avoid these 7 Roadblocks when communicating with God. See the table on the next page. Then, type this link in your web browser to access a digital copy of it:

http://sindynagel.com/index.php/7-roadblocks-free-infographic/

7 ROADBLOCKS TO HEARING GOD SPEAK

REMOVING THE BARRIERS BETWEEN YOU AND GOD
©SINDY NAGEL

	LIE	TRUTH	SCRIPTURE
DOUBT – The Enemy of Belief	God does *not* still speak today.	God's Holy Spirit, Who dwells in the hearts of believers, speaks to us.	John 16:13-15
	God speaks only to prophets, pastors, and spiritual leaders.	If you are a child of God, you can hear Him speak.	John 8:47
	I don't know if it's God's voice I hear.	The Lord is the Shepherd and you are His sheep who knows His voice.	John 10:2-4
FEAR – The Enemy of Confidence	The only thing God has to say to you is to convict you of your sin.	God speaks words of love, wisdom, peace, and encouragement.	Proverbs 2:5-6, 1 Cor. 2:7-16
	God will ask you to do something you don't want to do.	God created us to do good works He prepared in advance for us to do.	Ephesians 2:10
	God is full of wrath and fury for those who have sinned.	God rejoices over the sinner who repents and He pursues the lost.	Luke 15:7
PRIDE – The Enemy of Humility	I can take care of myself. I know what's best for me.	God will take care of you. He knows what's best for you, and has plans for you.	Isaiah 55:6-11, Jeremiah 29:11-14
	I am in control of my own life.	Christ controls all things.	Ephesians 1:17-22
	I am better than _____ because I _____. (Fill in the blanks.)	Exalt yourself & you'll be humbled. Humble your-self & God exalts you.	Philippians 2:3-11, Luke 14:11
WORRY – The Enemy of Trust	God won't provide for all my needs.	God will meet all your needs.	Philippians 4:19
	I can't trust God because He let me down in the past.	God is trustworthy; He never leaves you or forgets you.	Joshua 1:5
	I need to take care of things myself because God isn't.	God works all things together for your good.	Romans 8:28
BUSYNESS – The Enemy of Freedom	I don't have time to wait for God to speak to me.	There is a time for everything; a time to speak and a time to listen.	Ecclesiastes 3:1,7
	All these other activities I need to do are more urgent than time with God.	Spending time with God is our #1 priority.	Deuteronomy 5:7, Deut. 6:5-9
	Investing time in godly activities equals having a relationship with Jesus.	A relationship with Jesus is more than practicing good, religious activities.	John 15:3-10
DISOBEDIENCE – The Enemy of Righteousness	Your sins are too big for God to forgive.	When you confess your sin, God is faithful and just and will forgive it.	1 John 1:9
	You need to keep asking for forgiveness for the same sin.	The blood of Christ erases our sins, and God forgets them, so we should too.	Isaiah 43:18-19, Jeremiah 31:34
	God will *never* speak to you because of your sin or past.	God speaks to His children.	John 8:47, John 10:27
UNWILLINGNESS TO FORGIVE – The Enemy of Mercy	I can't forgive my brother or sister, he/she hurt me too deeply.	With God all things are possible.	Philippians 4:13, Matthew 19:26
	God doesn't expect me to forgive this one.	God requires that we forgive all those who trespass against us.	Mark 11:25, Colossians 3:13
	God will forgive me even if I don't forgive others.	God will forgive you *after* you forgive others.	Matthew 6:14-15

Purchase Sindy's other books on Amazon.com

**Manna for Today:
Bread from Heaven for Each Day**

ISBN: 978-1-4497-6704-4 (Paperback)
ISBN: 978-1-4497-6705-1 (Hardcover)
ISBN: 978-1-4497-6703-7 (Kindle)

Publisher: WestBow Press (A Division of Thomas Nelson)

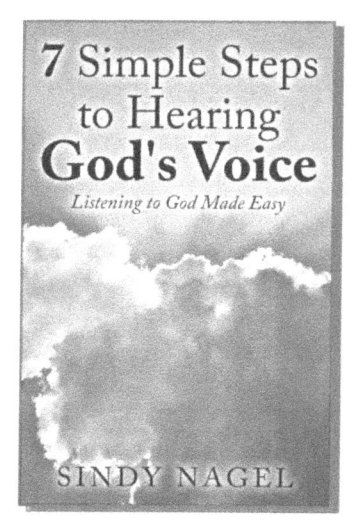

Hearing God's Voice Series (Book 1)

7 Simple Steps to Hearing God's Voice: Listening to God Made Easy

ISBN: 978-0-9969934-0-1 (Paperback)
ISBN: 978-0-9969934-7-0 (Kindle)
ISBN: 978-0-9969934-3-2 (Audio)

Hearing God's Voice Series

By Sindy Nagel

7 Simple Steps to Hearing God's Voice (Book 1)

7 Roadblocks to Hearing God Speak (Book 2)

Forthcoming:

7 Roles of the Holy Spirit

7 Rewards of Hearing God's Voice

7 Times to Listen to God

7 Places to Listen to God

7 Ways to Listen to God

Follow Sindy's Blog

www.sindynagel.com

Follow Sindy on Facebook and Twitter

www.facebook.com/SindyNagel.Author/

www.twitter.com/SindyNagel

See Sindy's Author Page on Amazon

http://www.amazon.com/Sindy-Nagel/e/B00BAJKYEM